MATHS PLUS

FROM HEINEMANN

YEAR 4

Key Lessons in Numeracy

Numbers and the Number System

GW00514849

Paul Broadbent

Kathryn Church

Heinemann

Heinemann Educational Publishers
Halley Court, Jordan Hill, Oxford, OX2 8EJ
a division of Reed Educational and Professional Publishing Ltd

Heinemann is a registered trademark of Reed Educational and Professional Publishing Ltd

Oxford Melbourne Auckland
Johannesburg Blantyre Gaborone
Ibadan Portsmouth (NH) Chicago

Acknowledgements

The publisher would like to thank the DfEE for permission to quote from the National Numeracy Strategy *Framework for teaching mathematics.*

First published 1999

04 03 02 01 00 99
10 9 8 7 6 5 4 3 2

Individual ISBN 0 435 02535 X
Key Stage 2 Omnibus Pack ISBN 0 435 02545 7
Complete Omnibus Pack ISBN 0 435 02550 3

Designed by Susan Clarke
Illustrated by David Mostyn
Cover design by Tinstar
Printed and bound in Great Britain

Contents

Introduction

The National Numeracy Strategy

Key Lessons in Numeracy is a series of books written to support teachers implementing the National Numeracy Strategy. *Numbers and the Number System Year 4* focuses on the 'Numbers and the Number System' strand of the National Numeracy Strategy 'Framework'. It provides a bank of 20 lessons for year 4 which each deal with key teaching objectives, including those that introduce mathematical content that may be 'new' to year 4 classes, but also giving support for topics that are known to be difficult to teach.

Each lesson aims to give teachers everything needed for a well structured, purposeful and successful lesson. In line with the recommendations of the National Numeracy Strategy, the lessons in *Numbers and the Number System Year 4* provide:

- support for direct teaching
- an emphasis on mental methods of calculation
- interactive involvement with the pupils through careful questioning
- lessons which are well paced and offer challenge
- a variety of activities to consolidate and extend understanding.

Resources

A range of resources will be useful as part of the interactive teaching approach promoted within *Numbers and the Number System Year 4*:

'Show me' activities involve pupils showing the answer by holding up a prop such as a digit card or fan number. In this way all pupils are involved and the teacher has a clear idea of their responses and understanding. This method also avoids individuals being singled out to respond orally. Resource sheets 1 (fan numbers) and 2 (digit cards), provided at the end of the book, can be photocopied for use with appropriate lessons.

The **counting stick** (a rule marked into 10 equal sections) is also referred to regularly as a teaching aid.

fan numbers

digit cards

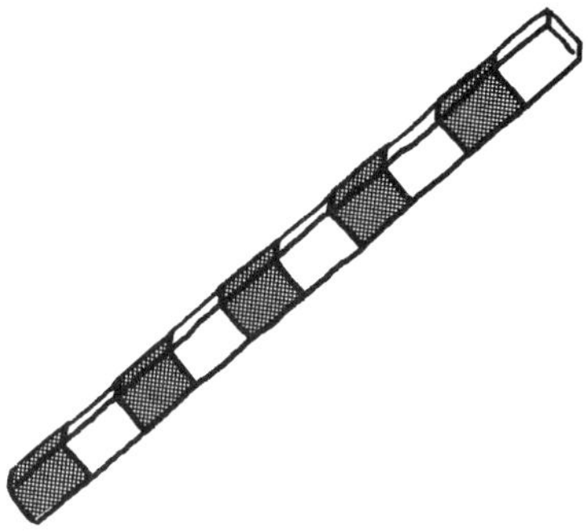

counting stick

Using this book

The National Numeracy Strategy recommends that each numeracy lesson should start with a 5–10 minute mental maths warm-up. A range of commercially produced resources are available from which you can choose activities for this section of the lesson. The focus within *Numbers and the Number System Year 4* is support for the main teaching session and pupil activities.

When planning teaching objectives on a medium-term or weekly basis the Numeracy 'Framework' should be the starting point. Once the teaching objectives have been chosen, the table on pp. 8–9 can be used to choose the appropriate lesson and topic. The intention within *Numbers and the Number System Year 4* is not to provide comprehensive coverage of the year 4 curriculum within a mere 20 lessons – that would clearly be impossible. Rather, it is to provide a starting point for teaching the most important aspects of the 'Framework'. A range of consolidation – both teaching and activity – will be needed, depending on the needs of individual classes and children.

A typical lesson plan is shown on p. 7, with the main sections labelled. The structure of each lesson follows a broadly similar format: a step-by-step description of the teaching followed by 3 photocopiable activities geared towards the needs of different ability groups. For each lesson, **Further activities** provide suggestions for follow-up work related to the topic.

lesson title

specific lesson objective

resources to prepare and organize before the lesson

previous stage of learning before this objective is taught

outline of pupil activity aimed at the majority of the class

outline of pupil activity aimed at higher attainers, or for an extension lesson

LESSON 3 Changing numbers by 1, 10, 100, 1000

Lesson objective

- to add or subtract 1, 10, 100 or 1000 to or from any integer, and count on or back in tens, hundreds or thousands, from any whole number up to 10 000

Language

- digit, more, less

Resources

- individual sets of arrow cards (Resource sheet 5), two dice (one marked 'more' on three faces and 'less' on the other three; the other marked 1 on one face, 10 on two faces, 100 on two faces and 1000 on the remaining face), **PCM3a, 3b, 3c**

Prior learning

- partitioning 4-digit numbers

Teaching *whole class: about 15 minutes*

- Explain to the children that this lesson is about using what they know about place value to make numbers bigger and smaller by addition or subtraction.
- Ask the children to start at 1234 and count in ones to 1245. Then ask them to start at 6474 and count back in ones to 6464. Ask the children to use their arrow cards to show you the answers to the following and explain any common misunderstandings:
  What is 1 more than 37? 6045? 809? What is 1 less than 512? 31? 3720? To find 1 less than 3720, we need to take away a unit, but we have no units. Look at the smallest arrow card (20). We can take 1 away from this. What does it give? (19) How can we make this with arrow cards? (10 and 9).
  Repeat this activity using other 3- and 4-digit numbers.
- Ask the children to start at 354 and count in tens to 424. Then ask them to count back in tens from 572 to 472. Ask the children to use their arrow cards to show you the answers to the following:
  What is 10 more than 59? 726? 1640? 2493? What is 10 less than 62? 806? 1300?
  Discuss the methods used and any difficulties the children experienced with some numbers, for example, 10 more than 2493. Repeat this activity using other 3- and 4-digit numbers.
- Ask the children to count on in steps of 100 from 630 to 1230, and then back in steps of 100 from 1528 to 928. Ask the children to use their arrow cards to show you the answers to the following:
  What is 100 more than 432? 3851? 2900? 1964? What is 100 less than 657? 1203? 5000? 2307?
  Discuss any difficulties, as before. Repeat this activity using other 3- and 4-digit numbers.
- Ask the children to count on in steps of 1000 from 263 to 7263, and then back in steps of 1000 from 9025 to 25. Ask the children to use their arrow cards to show you the answers to the following:
  What is 1000 more than 652? 3651? 2907? What is 1000 less than 5087? 1900? 5060?
  Repeat this activity using other 3- and 4-digit numbers.

18 **Key Lessons in Numeracy:** Numbers and the Number System Year 4

Activities *about 15 minutes*

Core (for whole class or average attainers)

Hand out **PCM3a**, explaining to the children that they will be making numbers bigger and smaller by adding or subtracting 1, 10, 100 or 1000. Before they begin, make sure they understand that they should fill in the missing numbers before completing the number sequences.

Extension (for extension lesson or higher attainers)

Give the children **PCM3b**, telling them that they will need their arrow cards to play a game. The game is played in pairs. Each player makes a 4-digit number using the arrow cards without revealing it to his or her opponent. Each player then takes it in turn to ask for a single digit, so Player A might say 'Give me your eights' to Player B who has the number 2582. Player B takes out the 80 card and puts it with their spare arrow cards, leaving the number 2502. Player A then adds 80 to their number, changing the arrow cards accordingly. So if A has 3146, is the number changed to 3226. The first player to go beyond 10 000, or to leave the opponent with 0, wins the game.

Support (for reinforcement lesson or lower attainers)

Hand out **PCM3c**, explaining to the children that they will be playing a game using the pre-prepared dice. Each player starts with the number 5432. They take turns to roll the two dice to make the number 1, 10, 100 or 1000 'more' or 'less' according to the instructions rolled. A running score should be kept by each player on the **PCM**. The + and – signs can be crossed out to show if the number should be increased or decreased. The first player to go beyond 9000 wins, but if a player goes below 0, they are out.

Plenary *whole class: about 10 minutes*

Write 2356 and 2376 on the board.

What do we have to add to the first number to make the second number? Repeat this using other pairs of numbers where the difference is a small number of either units or tens or hundreds or thousands.

Remind the children that they have learned more about place value today and that it should help them when they carry out calculations.

Further activities

- Each child sets up a constant on a calculator for adding or subtracting 1, 10, 100 or 1000 and looks at the patterns generated. For example, to set up a constant to repeatedly add 100, press *100 + + = 46* (or use any starting number). Keep pressing the equals sign to generate the sequence:
  146 246 346 446 546, and so on.
  To set up a constant to repeatedly subtract 1000, press: *1000 – – = 7845* (or use any starting number). Keep pressing the equals sign to generate the sequence:
  7845 6845 5845 4845, and so on.
  The children can record the sequences generated by using different constants.

Place value, ordering and rounding 19

key language to use and develop during the lesson

outline of pupil activity aimed at lower attainers, or for reinforcement lesson

plenary session to round up the lesson and reinforce the teaching point

further activities to follow up the lesson and to consolidate the understanding of the teaching objective

Match to Numeracy Framework

Year 4 teaching programme

Numbers and the number system	*lesson*	*lesson objectives*
Place value, ordering and rounding (whole numbers)		
• Read and write whole numbers to at least 10 000 in figures and words, and know what each digit represents.	1	to read and write numbers to at least 10 000 in figures and words and know what each digit represents
Partition numbers into thousands, hundreds, tens and ones.	2	to partition numbers into thousands, hundreds, tens and units
• Add/subtract 1, 10, 100 or 1000 to/from any integer and count on or back in tens, hundreds or thousands from any whole number up to 10 000.	3	to add or subtract 1, 10, 100 or 100 to or from any whole number, and count on or back in tens, hundreds or thousands, from any number up to 10 000
• Multiply or divide any integer up to 1000 by 10 (whole-number answers), and understand the effect.	4	to multiply or divide any whole number less than 1000 by 10 and understand the effect
Begin to multiply by 100.	4	see above
• Read and write the vocabulary of comparing and ordering numbers. **Use symbols correctly, including less than (<), greater than (>), equals (=).**	5	to compare and order numbers using appropriate vocabulary and use symbols correctly, including less than (<), greater than (>), equals (=)
Give one or more numbers lying between two given numbers and order a set of whole numbers less than 10 000.	6	to give one or more numbers lying between two given numbers, and order a set of whole numbers less than 10 000
• Read and write the vocabulary of estimation and approximation. Make and justify estimates up to about 250, and estimate a proportion.	7	to read and write the vocabulary of estimation and approximation, and make and justify estimates
Round any positive integer less than 1000 to the nearest 10 or 100.	8	to round any number less than 1000 to the nearest 10 or 100
• Recognize negative numbers in context (e.g. on a number line, on a temperature scale).	9	to recognize negative numbers in context
Properties of numbers and number sequences		
• Recognize and extend number sequences formed by counting from any number in steps of constant size, extending beyond zero when counting back: for example, count on in steps of 25 to 500, and then back to, say, –100.	10	to recognize and extend number sequences formed by counting on and back in steps of constant size, extending beyond 0 when counting back
• Recognize odd and even numbers up to 1000, and some of their properties, including the outcome of sums or differences of pairs of odd/even numbers.	11	to recognize odd and even numbers up to 1000 and some of their properties, including the outcomes of sums and differences of pairs of odd/even numbers
• Recognize multiples of 2, 3, 4, 5 and 10, up to tenth multiple.	12	to recognize multiples of 2, 3, 4, 5 and 10 up to the tenth multiple
Fractions and decimals		
• Use fraction notation. **Recognize simple fractions that are several parts of a whole,** such as $\frac{2}{3}$ or $\frac{5}{8}$**, and mixed numbers,** such as $5\frac{3}{4}$**, and**	13	to recognize simple fractions that are several parts of a whole, such as $\frac{2}{3}$ or $\frac{5}{8}$
• **recognize the equivalence of simple fractions** (e.g. fractions equivalent to $\frac{1}{2}$, $\frac{1}{4}$ or $\frac{3}{4}$)		
Identify two simple fractions with a total of 1 (e.g. $\frac{3}{10}$ and $\frac{7}{10}$)	15	to identify two simple fractions which have a total of 1, for example $\frac{3}{10}$ and $\frac{7}{10}$

Year 4 teaching programme
Numbers and the number system

	lesson	*lesson objectives*
• Order simple fractions: for example, decide whether fractions such as $\frac{3}{8}$ or $\frac{7}{10}$ are greater or less than one half	14	to order fractions, for example, decide whether fractions such as $\frac{3}{8}$ or $\frac{7}{10}$ are greater or less than $\frac{1}{2}$
• Begin to relate fractions to division and find simple fractions such as $\frac{1}{2}$, $\frac{1}{3}$, $\frac{1}{4}$, $\frac{1}{5}$, $\frac{1}{10}$... of numbers or quantities	16	to begin to relate fractions to division and find simple fractions of numbers or quantities
Find fractions such as $\frac{2}{3}$, $\frac{3}{4}$, $\frac{3}{5}$, $\frac{7}{10}$... of shapes		
• Begin to use ideas of simple proportion: for example, 'one for every ...' and 'one in every ...'	17	to begin to use ideas of simple proportion, for example, one for every and one in every
• Understand decimal notation and place value for tenths and hundredths, and use it in context. For example:	18	to understand the decimal notation for tenths to recognize the equivalence between the decimal and fraction forms of the tenths
order amounts of money; convert a sum of money such as £13·25 to pence, or a length such as 125 cm to metres;	19	to use decimal notation in the context of money to convert a sum of money such as £13·25 to pence
round a sum of money to the nearest pound	20	to round a sum of money to the nearest pound
• Recognize the equivalence between the decimal and fraction forms of one half and one quarter, and tenths such as 0·3	18	see above

Place value, ordering and rounding

LESSON 1 Reading and writing numbers to 10 000

Lesson objective

- to read and write numbers to at least 10 000 in figures and words and know what each digit represents

Language

- digit, names for numbers up to 10 000

Resources

- 4-spike abacus, individual fan numbers or digit cards (Resource sheets 1 and 2), **PCM1a, 1b, 1c**

Prior learning

- reading and writing numbers to at least 1000

Teaching ***whole class: about 15 minutes***

- Explain to the children that this lesson is about reading and writing numbers up to 10 000 in both figures and in words.
- Write a 4-digit number on the board in words and ask one of the children to read it. Then ask another child to write the number as a numeral.

  Show the children how the number on the board is represented on the abacus and remind them that the four columns represent thousands, hundreds, tens and units. Point to each digit in the numeral on the board as you explain this.
- Write a second 4-digit number on the board in words and ask one of the children to read it. Then ask another child to write the number as a numeral and a third to represent it on the abacus. Discuss any errors or misconceptions they make.
- Write a third 4-digit number on the board, but this time as a numeral. Ask one of the children to read the number, one to write it in words and one to show it on the abacus. Continue this activity for a few more 4-digit numbers, alternating between starting with a number in words and a number as a numeral, and including some numbers with zero hundreds, tens or units.
- Ask four children to come to the front of the class. Shuffle a set of digit cards and ask each child to pick one card. Then, with the help of the class, ask the children to make as many different numbers as they can using the four digits. (There are 24 permutations in total, so stop at ten different numbers to make it manageable.) As a number is said aloud, write it on the board. When ten numbers have been found, ask for the biggest number, the smallest number, a number with 3 tens, and so on.

Activities ***about 15 minutes***

Core (for whole class or average attainers)

Explain to the children that they will be practising writing numbers as both numerals and words. Give the children **PCM1a** and tell them that they should work out the number shown on each abacus and write it in both numerals and words.

Extension (for extension lesson or higher attainers)

Hand out copies of **PCM1b** and wait as the children to read the instructions. Make sure they understand that they are making different numbers from the four digit cards picked. They should show each number they make by placing counters onto the picture of the abacus. Each number is then written in their book, both as a word and a numeral.

Support (for reinforcement lesson or lower attainers)

Work with this group as they practise writing numbers in figures and words. Give each child a copy of **PCM1c** and ask them to find 4675 on the sheet. Discuss how they knew which number it was, and ask them to write the number in words. Then ask individual children to read out one of the numbers randomly, giving each child a turn. They then record each number in numerals or as a word, as appropriate.

Plenary

whole class: about 10 minutes

Write four different single digits on the board, one below the other. Ask the children to show you a number containing all four digits using their fan numbers or digit cards. Record on the board all the different numbers the children show, saying each as you do so. Do the children think there are any other possible numbers? Ask the children who did the 'Extension' activity how many different numbers they found using their four digits. Suggest that the children try making numbers from four digits at home to try to find the maximum number of numbers which can be made.

Discuss how they got on at home in the next lesson, making sure you include the effect that a zero has on the maximum number.

Further activities

- Play some place value games using a set of digit cards and empty recording boxes. Shuffle the cards and turn over the first digit to show the children. Ask them to decide where to write the digit in a row of four boxes – the aim being to make the largest number possible. Repeat until four digits have been shown. Then ask the children to read the numbers out and decide which is the largest. Repeat this with the children trying to make the smallest number possible. Decide whether to replace the digit cards once they have been used or to put them to one side.

Name: ....

1a

Reading and writing numbers to 10 000

Write these both as numbers and as words.

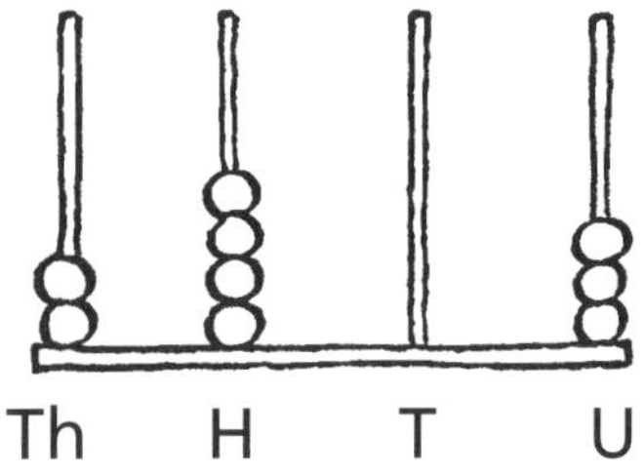

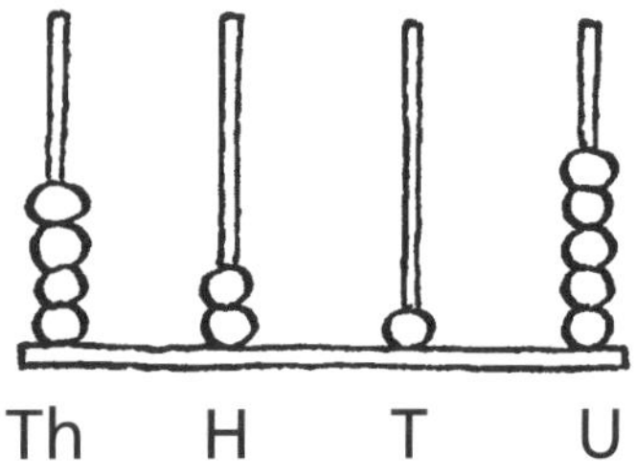

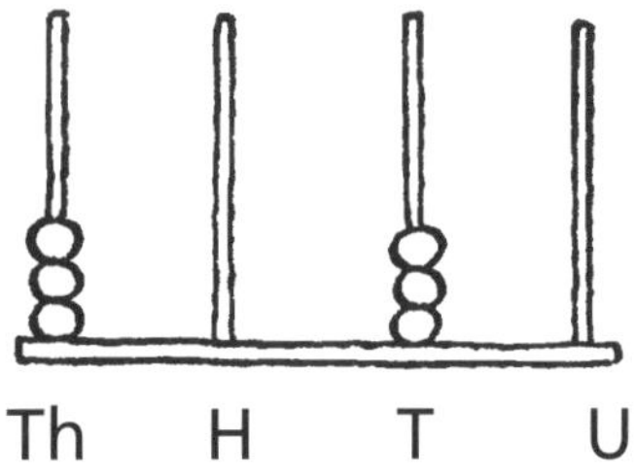

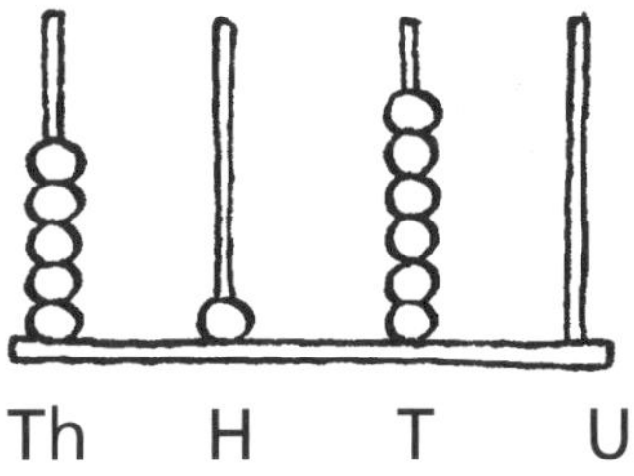

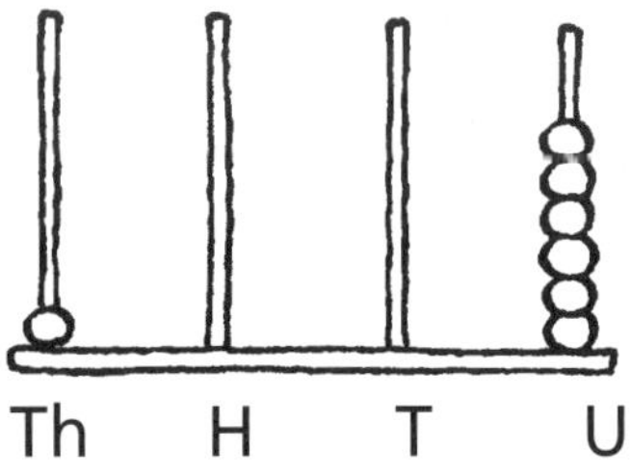

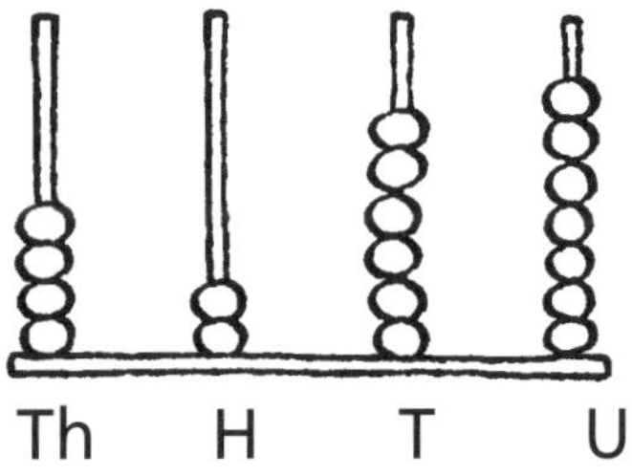

Name: ....

1b

Reading and writing numbers to 10 000

You need: some counters, 0–9 digit cards

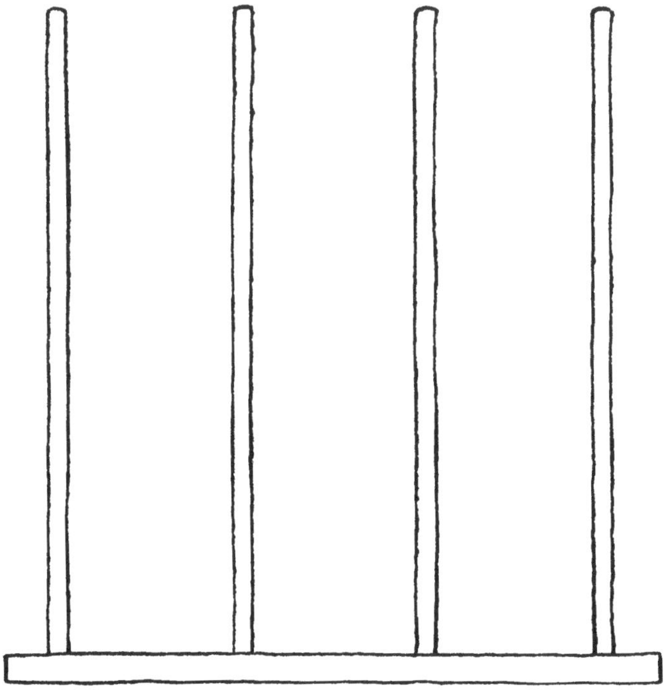

- Shuffle the digit cards.
- Pick any four cards.
- Make a 4-digit number from the cards. Place counters on the abacus to show the number.
- Write the number in your book as a word and a numeral.
- Make as many different numbers as you can from the four digits.

Name: ....

1c

Reading and writing numbers to 10 000

Write the missing numbers in words or figures.

2487	______________________
☐ four thousand and eighteen	☐ three thousand and forty
4250	______________________
☐ four thousand, two hundred and six	☐ two thousand
4675	______________________
☐ eight thousand and sixty-three	

LESSON 2 Partitioning 4-digit numbers

Lesson objective

- to partition numbers into thousands, hundreds, tens and units

Language

- digit, names for numbers up to 10 000

Resources

- a large set of arrow cards (for the teacher to use for demonstration, Resource sheet 5 enlarged), individual sets of arrow cards (Resource sheet 5), a list of about six numbers with partitioned equivalents on the board, for example:
  5274 = 5000 + __ + 70 + 4
  3509 = ___ + 500 + 9
  4291 = 4000 + 200 +__ + 1
  7032 = 7000 + __ + 2,
  decahedral dice numbered 0–9, digit cards (Resource sheets 1 and 2), **PCM2a, 2b, 2c**

Prior learning

- partitioning 3-digit numbers

Teaching *whole class: about 15 minutes*

- Explain to the children they are going to learn more about place value in 4-digit numbers in this lesson.
- Show the children a 4-digit number using the large set of arrow cards (with four different numbers). Point out that this is a 4-digit number because it has four separate symbols which we call *digits*. Ask them what each digit represents before taking out the appropriate card to reveal the value of the digit. Repeat this for other 4-digit numbers.
- Give the children the individual sets of arrow cards. Say a variety of 2-, 3- and 4-digit numbers, asking the children to show them with their cards. Discuss the value of individual digits in the numbers, encouraging the children to check each answer by removing the appropriate card. Then use prompts, such as:

  Show me a number which has 5 tens, 8 hundreds, 3 thousands.

  Show me a number with 6 thousands and 6 tens.

  Show me any number greater than 6000, with digits that total 10.

  (For example: 6121.)
- Reveal the list of equations on the board and ask the children to show you the missing numbers using their arrow cards.

Activities *about 15 minutes*

Core (for whole class or average attainers)

Give the children **PCM2a**, describing how they will be identifying numbers from pictures of separate arrow cards. Make sure they understand that the second part of the activity involves writing numbers on arrow cards to separate the value of their digits.

Extension (for extension lesson or higher attainers)

Explain to the children that they will be playing games in pairs using the decahedral dice. Hand out **PCM2b**. Players take turns to roll the dice and record the number in one of the four boxes in Game 1. The four boxes represent a 4-digit number. Each player has four turns until their number is complete, and the player with the largest number wins. Remind the children to consider their strategy as they play – that a high number is better to place in the thousands or hundreds, and a low number in the tens or ones. Game 2 is played in the same way, but with the smallest number winning. Again, remind them of the strategy of placing high and low numbers. In Game 3, each player takes eight turns to make two 4-digit numbers before adding them together. The player with the highest total wins.

All three games can be extended by each player choosing whether to keep the number rolled on the dice or give it to their partner. Players continue to throw the dice alternately until both players have 4-digit numbers, even if one has already completed theirs.

Support (for reinforcement lesson or lower attainers)

Provide the children with **PCM2c**. The games are similar to those on the 'Extension' activity and can be introduced at the same time. Rather than using decahedral dice, however, the children will randomly pick their digits from digit cards (the cards might be face down, or the children shut their eyes). The first two games involve making the largest and smallest 3-digit numbers, while the task of Games 3 and 4 is to make the largest and smallest 4-digit numbers.

Plenary

whole class: about 10 minutes

Write the number 5026 on the board. Ask the children to use their arrow cards to show you this number. Ask them what they notice about the 0 (there is no hundreds arrow card). Repeat the activity using other numbers with one or two zeros, asking the children both to make the number and to say it.

Further activities

- Play 'Make 10 000', a calculator game to be played in pairs. Each player puts any number into their calculator between 1000 and 5000 without seeing their partner's number. Player A asks for a digit from Player B, which is given as a thousand, hundred, ten or unit value. This is then taken away from Player B's number and added to Player A's number on the calculator. If there is no digit to take, they miss that go. For example:
  Player A, number is 2563
  Player B, number is 3419
  Player A: Can I have your fours?
  Player B: Yes – I have 400.
  Player A now has 2563 + 400 = 2963
  Player B now has 3419 – 400 = 3019
  The game is continued until one player wins by reaching 10 000 or loses by reaching 0.
- Play 'Arrow card bingo'. Each player makes a 4-digit number with their arrow cards. The teacher places a full set of arrow cards (ThHTU) in a bag and takes one card out at random. This is shown to the class and the number called out. For example, 'four hundred' (400). Children whose 4-digit number includes 400 remove the 400 card and place it in front of them. This is repeated and continued until a player has had all four arrow cards called out. This player shouts 'Bingo!' and is the winner.

Name: ....

2a

Partitioning 4-digit numbers

Write the numbers the arrow cards show.

4000, 6, 500, 20 ☐	60, 7, 200, 5000 ☐	900, 40, 2, 1000 ☐
1000, 7, 900, 10 ☐	8000, 400, 60, 2 ☐	600, 7, 9000, 50 ☐
80, 2000, 200, 4 ☐	8000, 9, 30, 500 ☐	6, 70, 100, 4000 ☐

Show these numbers on the arrow cards.

4185 →	☐☐☐☐	+	☐☐☐	+	☐☐	+	☐
6291 →	☐☐☐☐	+	☐☐☐	+	☐☐	+	☐
5229 →	☐☐☐☐	+	☐☐☐	+	☐☐	+	☐
6814 →	☐☐☐☐	+	☐☐☐	+	☐☐	+	☐
2971 →	☐☐☐☐	+	☐☐☐	+	☐☐	+	☐
9846 →	☐☐☐☐	+	☐☐☐	+	☐☐	+	☐

Name: ....

2b

Partitioning 4-digit numbers

You need: 10-sided dice (numbered 0–9), 0–9 digit cards

Follow the instructions the teacher gives you.

Game 1

Largest number

Game 2

Smallest number

Game 3

Largest total

+

Name: ....

2c

Partitioning 4-digit numbers

You need: 0–9 digit cards

Follow the instructions the teacher gives you.

Game 1

Largest number

Game 2

Smallest number

Game 3

Largest number

Game 4

Smallest number

LESSON 3 Changing numbers by 1, 10, 100, 1000

Lesson objective

- to add or subtract 1, 10, 100 or 1000 to or from any integer, and count on or back in tens, hundreds or thousands, from any whole number up to 10 000

Language

- digit, more, less

Resources

- individual sets of arrow cards (Resource sheet 5), two dice (one marked 'more' on three faces and 'less' on the other three; the other marked 1 on one face, 10 on two faces, 100 on two faces and 1000 on the remaining face), **PCM3a, 3b, 3c**

Prior learning

- partitioning 4-digit numbers

Teaching *whole class: about 15 minutes*

- Explain to the children that this lesson is about using what they know about place value to make numbers bigger and smaller by addition or subtraction.
- Ask the children to start at 1234 and count in ones to 1245. Then ask them to start at 6474 and count back in ones to 6464. Ask the children to use their arrow cards to show you the answers to the following and explain any common misunderstandings:

  What is 1 more than 37? 6045? 809? What is 1 less than 512? 31? 3720? To find 1 less than 3720, we need to take away a unit, but we have no units. Look at the smallest arrow card (20). We can take 1 away from this. What does it give? (19) How can we make this with arrow cards? (10 and 9).

  Repeat this activity using other 3- and 4-digit numbers.
- Ask the children to start at 354 and count in tens to 424. Then ask them to count back in tens from 572 to 472. Ask the children to use their arrow cards to show you the answers to the following:

  What is 10 more than 59? 726? 1640? 2493? What is 10 less than 62? 806? 1300?

  Discuss the methods used and any difficulties the children experienced with some numbers, for example, 10 more than 2493. Repeat this activity using other 3- and 4-digit numbers.
- Ask the children to count on in steps of 100 from 630 to 1230, and then back in steps of 100 from 1528 to 928. Ask the children to use their arrow cards to show you the answers to the following:

  What is 100 more than 432? 3851? 2900? 1964? What is 100 less than 657? 1203? 5000? 2307?

  Discuss any difficulties, as before. Repeat this activity using other 3- and 4-digit numbers.
- Ask the children to count on in steps of 1000 from 263 to 7263, and then back in steps of 1000 from 9025 to 25. Ask the children to use their arrow cards to show you the answers to the following:

  What is 1000 more than 652? 3651? 2907? What is 1000 less than 5087? 1900? 5060?

  Repeat this activity using other 3- and 4-digit numbers.

Activities

about 15 minutes

Core (for whole class or average attainers)

Hand out **PCM3a**, explaining to the children that they will be making numbers bigger and smaller by adding or subtracting 1, 10, 100 or 1000. Before they begin, make sure they understand that they should fill in the missing numbers before completing the number sequences.

Extension (for extension lesson or higher attainers)

Give the children **PCM3b**, telling them that they will need their arrow cards to play a game. The game is played in pairs. Each player makes a 4-digit number using the arrow cards without revealing it to his or her opponent. Each player then takes it in turn to ask for a single digit, so Player A might say 'Give me your eights' to Player B who has the number 2582. Player B takes out the 80 card and puts it with their spare arrow cards, leaving the number 2502. Player A then adds 80 to their number, changing the arrow cards accordingly. So if A has 3146, is the number changed to 3226. The first player to go beyond 10 000, or to leave the opponent with 0, wins the game.

Support (for reinforcement lesson or lower attainers)

Hand out **PCM3c**, explaining to the children that they will be playing a game using the pre-prepared dice. Each player starts with the number 5432. They take turns to roll the two dice to make the number 1, 10, 100 or 1000 'more' or 'less' according to the instructions rolled. A running score should be kept by each player on the **PCM**. The + and – signs can be crossed out to show if the number should be increased or decreased. The first player to go beyond 9000 wins, but if a player goes below 0, they are out.

Plenary

whole class: about 10 minutes

Write 2356 and 2376 on the board.

What do we have to add to the first number to make the second number? Repeat this using other pairs of numbers where the difference is a small number of either units or tens or hundreds or thousands.

Remind the children that they have learned more about place value today and that it should help them when they carry out calculations.

Further activities

- Each child sets up a constant on a calculator for adding or subtracting 1, 10, 100 or 1000 and looks at the patterns generated. For example, to set up a constant to repeatedly add 100, press *100 + + = 46* (or use any starting number). Keep pressing the equals sign to generate the sequence:
  146 246 346 446 546, and so on.

  To set up a constant to repeatedly subtract 1000, press: *1000 – – = 7845* (or use any starting number). Keep pressing the equals sign to generate the sequence:
  7845 6845 5845 4845, and so on.
  The children can record the sequences generated by using different constants.

Name: ....

3a

Changing numbers by 1, 10, 100, 1000

Write the answers.

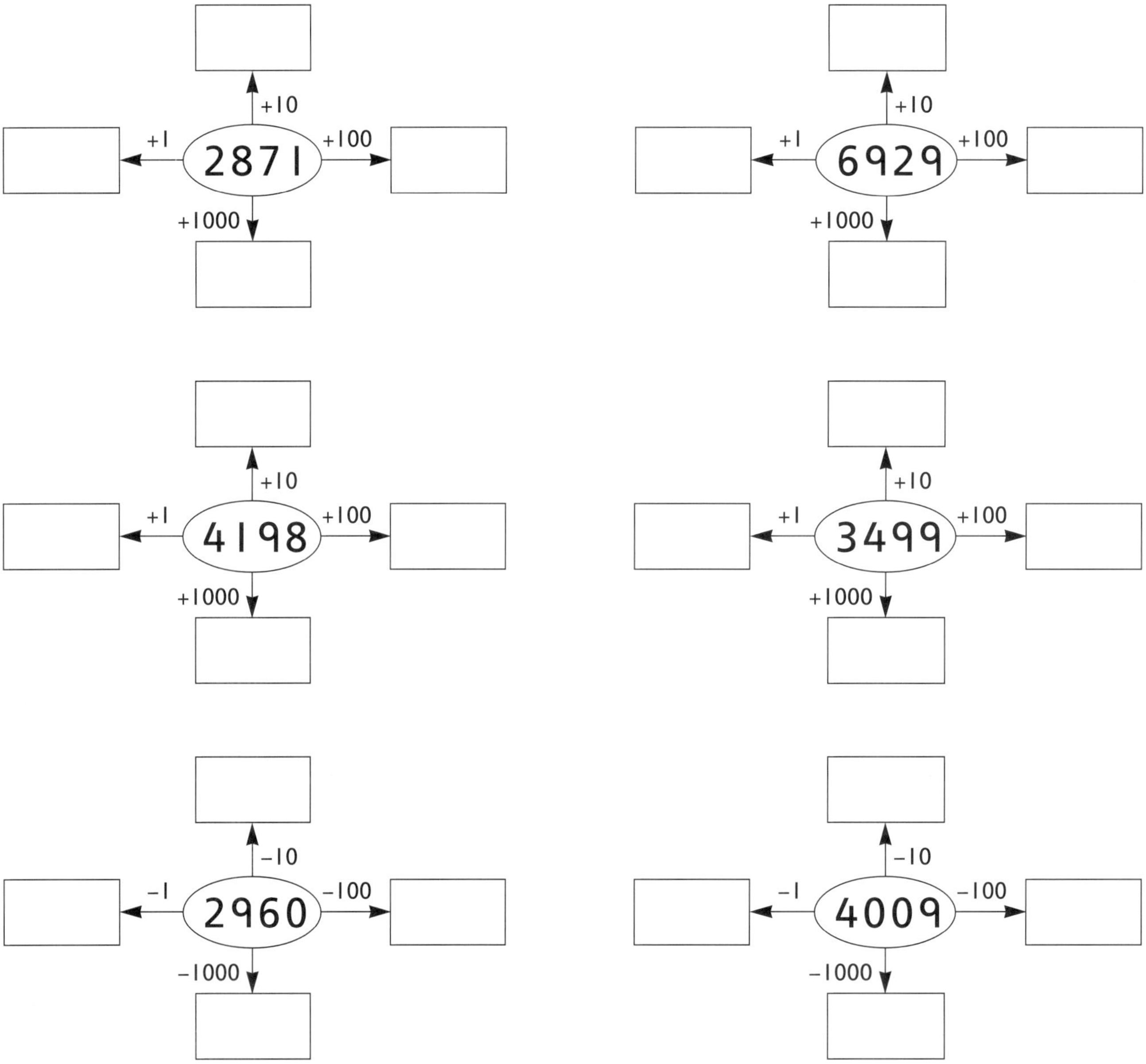

Now continue these sequences.

2805	2705	2605	______	______	8003	8002	8001	______	______
3148	3138	3128	______	______	6799	6899	6999	______	______
6056	6057	6058	______	______	8108	7108	6108	______	______
1694	2694	3694	______	______	5964	5974	5984	______	______

Name: ....

3b

Changing numbers by 1, 10, 100, 1000

You will need:
arrow cards

The aim is to get more than 10 000 before your partner.

Follow the instructions the teacher gives you.

GAME 1

Number	+ / –

GAME 2

Number	+ / –

GAME 3

Number	+ / –

Name: ....

3c

Changing numbers by 1, 10, 100, 1000

You will need:
special dice

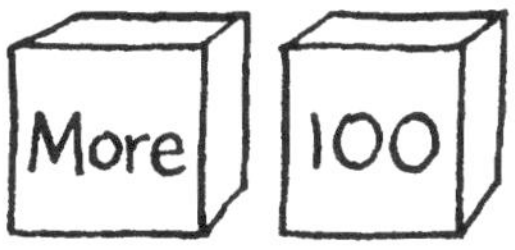

The aim is to reach 9000 before your partner.

Follow the instructions the teacher gives you.

GAME 1

Number		more / less
5432	+ –	
	+ –	
	+ –	
	+ –	
	+ –	
	+ –	
	+ –	
	+ –	
	+ –	
	+ –	

GAME 2

Number		more / less
5432	+ –	
	+ –	
	+ –	
	+ –	
	+ –	
	+ –	
	+ –	
	+ –	
	+ –	
	+ –	

GAME 3

Number		more / less
5432	+ –	
	+ –	
	+ –	
	+ –	
	+ –	
	+ –	
	+ –	
	+ –	
	+ –	
	+ –	

LESSON 4 Multiplying and dividing by 10

Lesson objective

- to multiply or divide any whole number less than 1000 by 10 (whole number answers) and understand the effect

Language

- multiply, digits, place (to describe the position of digits in a number)

Resources

- individual sets of digit cards with at least three zero cards (Resource sheet 2), **PCM4a, 4b, 4c**

Prior learning

- multiplying and dividing by 10 (introduced as a calculating strategy in Year 3 for single digits and multiples of 10)

Teaching *whole class: about 15 minutes*

- Explain to the children that this lesson is about multiplying and dividing numbers by 10.
- ***What is 8 multiplied by 10? What is 80 multiplied by 10? What is 4 multiplied by 10? What is 40 multiplied by 10?***

  What happens when we multiply a number by 10?

  Firmly establish that the digits move one place to the left and that the empty place in the units column is filled by 0. (Make sure the children do not still have the misconception that 'You put 0 on the end when you multiply by 10' this must be made very clear in this lesson to prevent errors.)

  So what is 800 multiplied by 10? What is 400 multiplied by 10? What is 15 multiplied by 10? What is 150 multiplied by 10?

  Record the last four answers on the board, pointing out how, in each case, all the digits have moved one place to the left. Emphasize that in *15 × 10*, the 10 becomes 100, the 5 becomes 50 and the empty units space is filled with 0. Now ask the children to multiply more 2- and 3-digit numbers by 10 and record the calculations on the board.
- ***What is 80 divided by 10? What is 800 divided by 10? What is 8000 divided by 10?***

  What happens when we divide a number by 10?

  Firmly establish that the digits move one place to the right.

  So what is 120 divided by 10? What is 350 divided by 10? What is 4200 divided by 10?

  Record the answers to these on the board, pointing out how, in each case, all the digits have moved one place to the right. Emphasize that in *120 ÷ 10*, the 100 becomes 10, the 20 becomes 2 and the 0 disappears because there is no longer an empty units place. Now ask the children to divide more 3- and 4-digit multiples of 10 by 10 and record the calculations on the board.

Activities *about 15 minutes*

Core (for whole class or average attainers)

Explain to the children that they will be using **PCM4a** to practise multiplying and dividing numbers by 10. Point out that they should look at each abacus and write its number in the box. They then draw beads on the corresponding empty abacus to show the effect of multiplying or dividing by 10 and write the numbers down. The full calculation should then be written out in their books.

Extension (for extension lesson or higher attainers)

Give the children **PCM4b**. Tell them that they can find their way through the maze by following the instructions to multiply by 10 or 100, or divide by 10. Suggest that they work in pencil, as it may take several attempts before the route is completed. There is a second maze for them to put in their own numbers and make up their own route. If necessary, remind the children how to multiply a number by 100, by multiplying by 10 and 10 again.

Support (for reinforcement lesson or lower attainers)

Working with this group, show them **PCM4c** and go through the first example with them.

How many hundreds are there? 1 hundred multiplied by 10 is 1000. Write the 1 in the thousands column.

How many tens are there? 3 tens multiplied by 10 is 300. Write the 3 in the hundreds column.

How many units are there? No units, so write a 0 in the tens and the units column. So, 130 multiplied by 10 is 1300.

Make sure they understand the process by asking them to work through the second example, explaining their working. Then work through the first example of dividing by 10, in the same way. The last box in each row is open for children to choose their own starting number. They then answer some multiplication and division calculations in their books.

Plenary

whole class: about 10 minutes

Provide the children with a selection of context questions involving multiplication and division, such as:

If I have twenty-five 10p coins, how much money do I have?

If I buy a box of ten pencils for £3·20, how much does one pencil cost?

(This example may need changing to 320p to simplify it for some children.) Ask

Further activities

- Each child sets up a constant on a calculator for multiplying or dividing by 10 and looks at the patterns generated. For example, to set up a constant to repeatedly multiply by 10, press: *10 × × = 23* (or use any starting number). Keep pressing the equals sign to generate the sequence:
  23 230 2300 23 000, and so on.

  To set up a constant to repeatedly divide by 10, press: *10 ÷ ÷ = 3000* (or use any starting number). Keep pressing the equals sign to generate the sequence:
  3000 300 30 3
  Discuss the decimal numbers that are generated with the children.

Name: ....

4a

Multiplying and dividing by 10

Write the number shown on each abacus.
Multiply or divide the number by 10 and
draw the correct number of beads on the blank abacus.

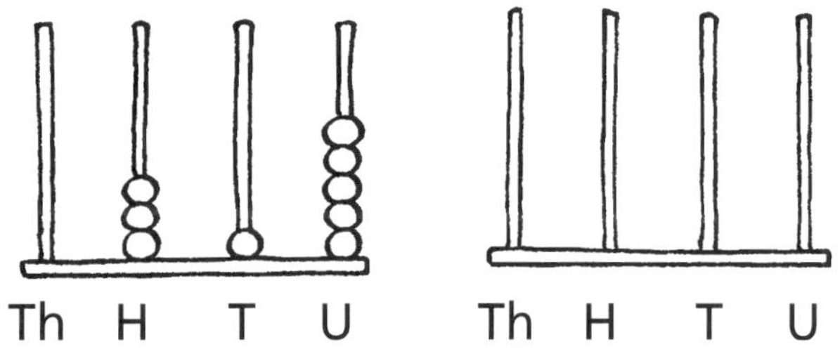

× 10 =

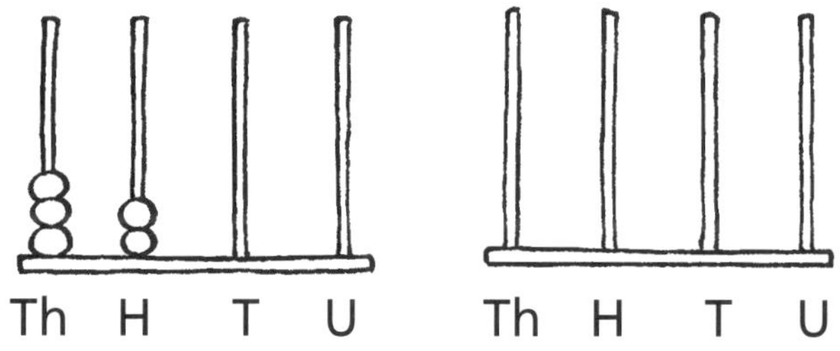

÷ 10 =

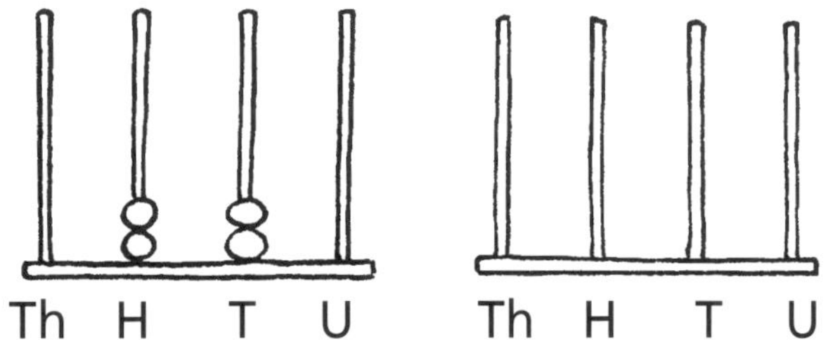

× 10 =

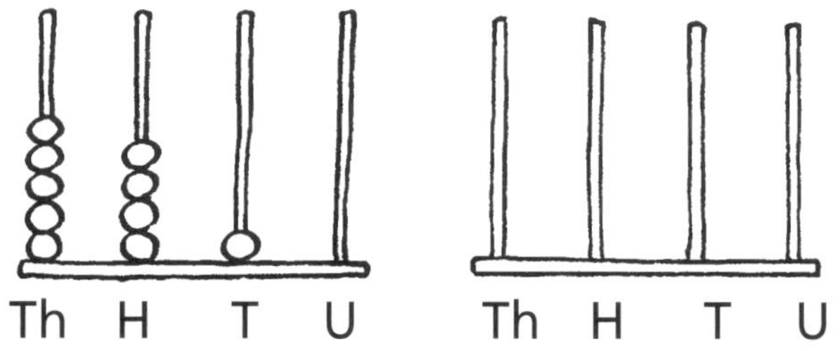

÷ 10 =

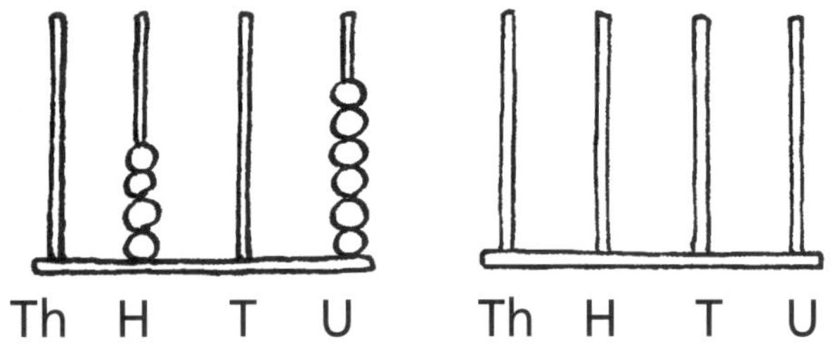

× 10 –

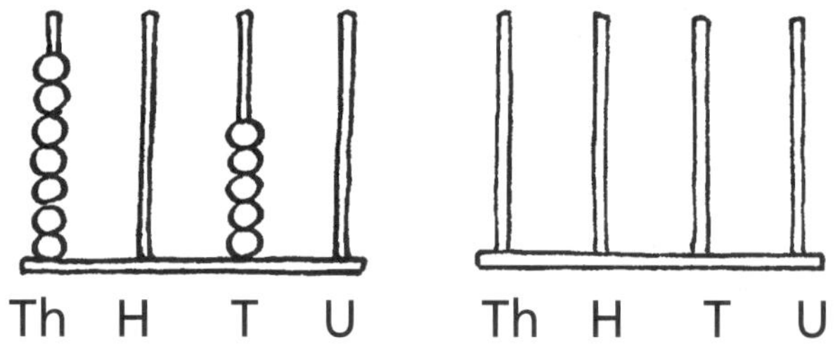

÷ 10 =

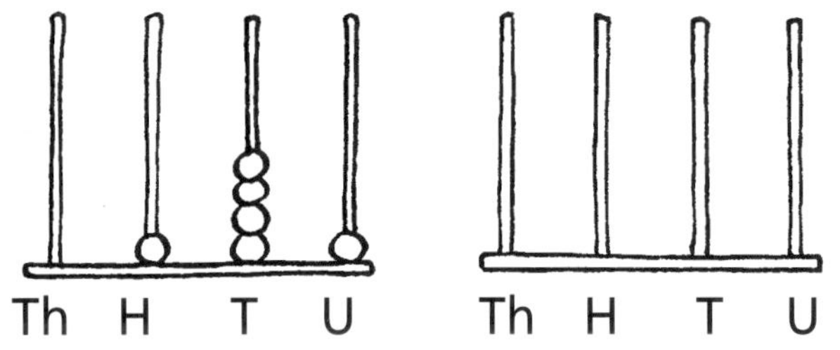

× 10 =

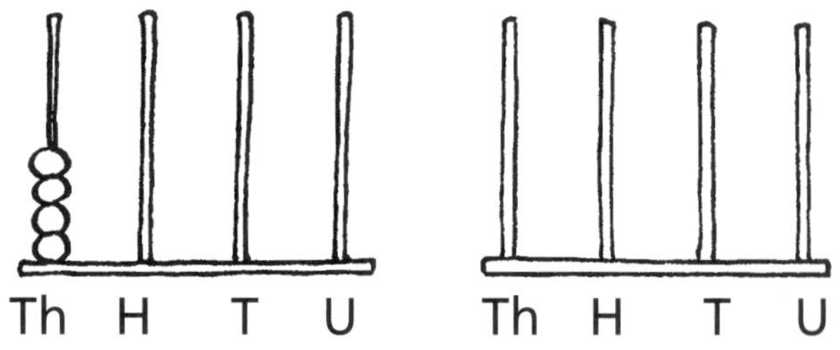

÷ 10 =

Name: ....

4b

Multiplying and dividing by 10

Follow the route through the maze. Colour the correct squares as you go.

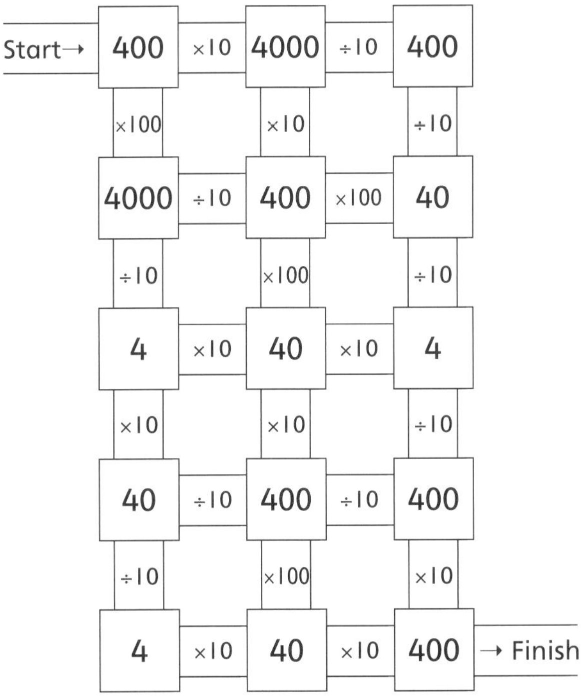

Now make up your own maze.

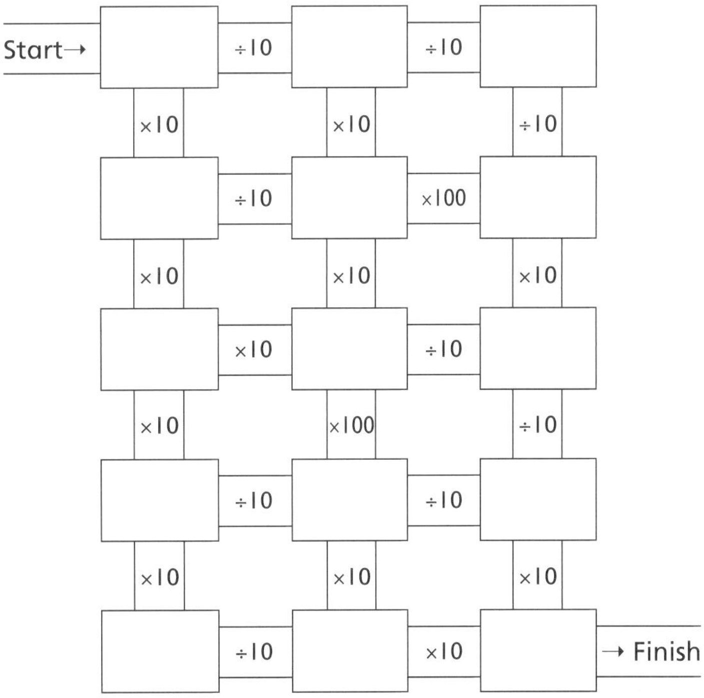

Name: ....

4c

Multiplying and dividing by 10

Complete these calculations.

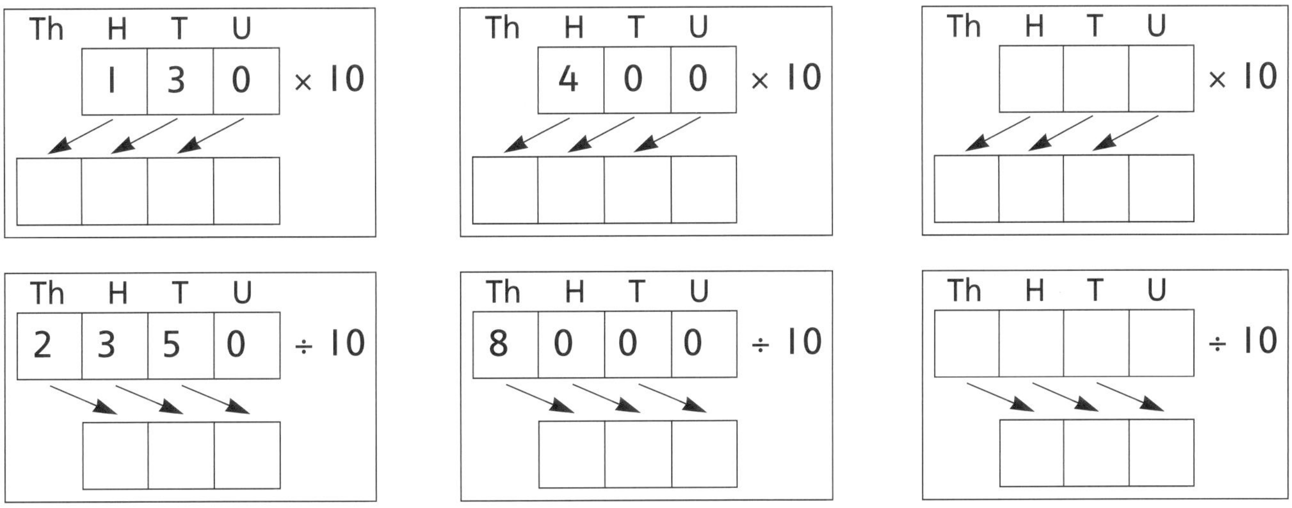

Answer these: 20 × 10 = 180 × 10 = 6000 ÷ 10 = 1840 ÷ 10 =

LESSON 5 Using symbols

Lesson objective

- to use the vocabulary of comparing and ordering numbers and use symbols correctly, including less than (<), greater than (>), equals (=)

Language

- greater than, more than, less than, fewer than

Resources

- a vertical list of the following words on the board:
  plus, subtract, multiplied by, divided by, equals
  a set of digit cards (Resource sheet 1) in a fun container such as a hat, **PCM5a, 5b, 5c**

Prior learning

- using + – × ÷ and = signs to record calculations and recognizing the use of a symbol to stand for an unknown number
- understanding and using numbers to at least 10 000

Teaching *whole class: about 20 minutes*

- Explain to the children that this lesson is about using symbols to compare numbers. Remind them that symbols are used in mathematics as a short way of presenting information. Ask someone to read the list of words on the board. Ask children to explain what each of the words means, then to write the appropriate mathematical sign beside each word.
- Tell the children that they are going to learn two new symbols today, one which means 'is greater than' and one which means 'is less than'. Write *greater than* and *less than* below the other words on the list.

  What does 'greater' than mean?

  Establish that it means more than and provide an example, such as 57 is greater than 50. Write the statement on the board with the symbol as: *57 > 50*, and explain that this symbol means *is greater than*.
- ***What does 'less' than mean?***

  Establish that it means fewer than and provide an example such as 20 is less than 40. Write the statement on the board with the symbol as: *20 < 40*, and explain that this symbol means *is less than*.
- Focus the children's attention on the two symbols, pointing out that each is rather like an arrow head, with the narrow end pointing to the smaller number and the wide end pointing to the bigger number.

  We 'read' the symbol from left to right, so the narrow end to the left means 'is less than' and the wide end to the left means 'is greater than'.

  Record the two new symbols beside the appropriate words on the list.
- Ask a child to write a 3-digit number on the board. Ask another child to write another 3-digit number beside the first, but leaving a space between, for example, 345 367.

  Is 345 less than 367 or greater than 367? So which symbol can we put between the two numbers?

  Ask another child to write in the appropriate symbol. Read the statement to the children aloud as:

  345 is less than 367.

- Write the other symbol on the board, for example, >, and ask the children to say what it means. Ask a child to supply a 4-digit number and write it in front of the symbol, then ask the class to supply other numbers which could be placed after the symbol to make the statement true. Record one of the numbers.
- Repeat both activities a few times using 3- and 4-digit numbers until you feel that the children understand.
- Draw two sets of four boxes on the board with > between each set. Read this out as 'a number is greater than another number'. Show the children the set of digit cards, making sure that they realize there are 10 cards containing the digits 0 to 9. Explain to the children that you are going to build up two 4-digit numbers, one on each side of the symbol, by taking digit cards out of the hat one by one. The children have to decide which box to write the digit in. Emphasize that the first 4-digit number must be greater than the second one.

  Draw out a digit card, show the class and ask a child to write the digit in a box of their choice. Do not replace the card in the hat. Continue until all 8 boxes contain digits, encouraging the children to think carefully about where to place digits to make the statement true. Emphasize the importance of comparing the value of thousands, and repeat the activity using the other sign.

Activities

about 20 minutes

Core (for whole class or average attainers)

Give the children **PCM5a**, and explain that they will be rearranging sets of four given digits to make different numbers. They then write these numbers in the boxes so that the statements are true. Complete the first example with them, drawing their attention to the help box at the top of the sheet.

Extension (for extension lesson or higher attainers)

Explain to the children they will be playing a game using **PCM5b**. Read through the rules with them and make sure they understand how to play. Once they have played a few times, ask them if they can think of any rule changes that could alter the game. They can then try out their variations on the game.

Support (for reinforcement lesson or lower attainers)

Hand out **PCM5c**, pointing out to the children that they are going to make statements true using < and > before writing in numbers to make some statements true. Go through the first few examples with this group, reminding them of the meaning of the two symbols.

Plenary

whole class: about 10 minutes

Repeat the digit card activity used in the teaching session, but this time replace the digits in the hat after each one is drawn out. Ask the children to comment on the effect this has on the game. Remind them that they have learned how to use two new mathematical symbols today.

Further activities

- Make a set of cards which reflect the language and symbols included in the lesson, half of which have a symbol, the other half of which have the corresponding words. Use the cards to play games such as 'Snap' and 'Pelmanism'.
- Using a given a set of numbers, and symbols such as + − × ÷ = > <, ask the children to write as many true statements as possible.

Name: ....

5a

Using symbols

Remember:
> greater than
< less than

Rearrange these digits to make three true statements.

4 6 5 8

☐☐☐☐ > ☐☐☐☐ ☐☐☐☐ < ☐☐☐☐

☐☐☐☐ > ☐☐☐☐ > ☐☐☐☐

Now use these digits to make three true statements.

2 9 7 3

☐☐☐☐ > ☐☐☐☐ > ☐☐☐☐ < ☐☐☐☐

☐☐☐☐ < ☐☐☐☐ > ☐☐☐☐ < ☐☐☐☐

Write a possible missing number for each of these.

7149 > ☐ > 7438 2005 < ☐ > 2904

6148 < ☐ < 6153 4852 > ☐ < 4621

9708 < ☐ > 3294 8204 > ☐ > 8198

Name: ....

5b

Using symbols

A game for two players.

You need: digit cards 0–9

0 1 2 3 4 5
6 7 8 9 0

- Shuffle the cards and place them face down.
- You and you partner take turns to pick a card and place it in one of the columns: Th H T U.
- Once in place, the cards cannot be moved.
- The winner is the player with the largest 4-digit number.
- Play several games. Is there a strategy for winning the game?

TH	H	T	U

Name: ....

5c

Using symbols

Write the signs > or < to make these statements true.

128 ☐ 144 809 ☐ 611 229 ☐ 290

2149 ☐ 2408 3914 ☐ 3099 6152 ☐ 6083

9462 ☐ 4993 5704 ☐ 5741 3219 ☐ 3129

Now write a possible missing number for each of these.

385 > ☐ > 314 296 > ☐ < 241 529 < ☐ < 711

609 > ☐ < 432 481 < ☐ > 637 804 > ☐ > 798

LESSON 6 Comparing and ordering numbers

Lesson objective

- to give one or more numbers lying between two given numbers, and order a set of whole numbers less than 10 000

Language

- less than, greater than, between, smallest, largest

Resources:

- large counting stick for the teacher, individual fan numbers or digit cards (Resource sheets 1 and 2), **PCM6a, 6b, 6c**

Prior learning

- partitioning 4-digit numbers
- comparing and ordering 3-digit numbers

Teaching

whole class: about 15 minutes

- Explain to the children that this lesson is about ordering and comparing the size of numbers.
- Hold up the counting stick so the whole class can see it and explain that the left-hand end, (as the children see it), is 0 and the right-hand end is 10 000.

  What is the middle number?

  Ask the children how they know – explaining that the whole stick represents 10 000, so each section represents 1000.

  Point to each tenth mark in order and ask the children to name the numbers.

  Where will I find 7500? Where is 3050?
- Tell them that the counting stick now represents a different range of numbers – the left-hand side is 5000 and the right-hand side is 6000.

  What is the middle number now?

  Point to each tenth mark in order and ask the children to name the numbers.

  Where will I find 5050? Where is 5690? Give me a number which is between 5200 and 5300.

  Now give me a number which is less than this. Greater than this.

  (Point to the marks on the stick.)
- Explain that the range has changed again so that the left-hand side is 3000 and the right-hand side is 3100.

  What is the middle number now?

  Point to each tenth mark in order and ask the children to name the numbers.

  Where can I find 3025? Where is 3099? Give me a number which is between 3030 and 3040.

  Now give me a number which is less than this. Greater than this.

  (Point to the marks on the stick.)
- Write 5312 and 5321 on the board.

  Which is the greater number? How do you know?

  Make sure they compare the value of the thousands, hundreds, tens and units.

  Use your fan numbers or digit cards to show me a number which is between these two numbers.

  Now repeat this activity using other pairs of 4-digit numbers.

Activities

about 20 minutes

Core (for whole class or average attainers)

Hand out **PCM6a**. Tell the children that they will be filling in missing numbers on number lines and putting sets of 4-digit numbers in order of size, starting with the smallest, and writing them in their books.

Extension (for extension lesson or higher attainers)

Give the children **PCM6b**. Explain that they will be making as many 4-digit numbers as possible from a given set of digits. Make sure they understand that they have to write the numbers in order of size.

Support (for reinforcement lesson or lower attainers)

Provide the children with **PCM6c**. Point out that the activity involves finding all the whole numbers which come between two given numbers. Work through the first example with the group and watch as they complete it to ensure they understand that they need to find all the numbers. Children who find this difficult should be encouraged to count from the smaller number to the larger and record all those between. Explain that when all the examples are finished they can make up some similar puzzles for a partner to solve.

Plenary

whole class: about 5 minutes

Using their fan numbers or digit cards, ask the children to show you a number which is:

Greater than 4517.

Less than 1010.

1 less than 2600.

Between 5260 and 5270.

The smallest number between 3995 and 4002. (3996)

Half-way between 6195 and 6205.

The largest whole number less than 8500. (8499)

And so on.

Explain to the children that they can now use all the numbers up to 10 000.

Further activities

- Play some place value games using a set of digit cards and empty recording boxes. Shuffle the cards and turn over the first digit to show the children. Ask them to decide where to write the digit in a row of four boxes – the aim being to make the largest number possible. Repeat until four digits have been shown. Then ask the children to read the numbers out and decide which is the largest. Repeat this with the children trying to make the smallest number possible. Decide whether to replace the digit cards once they have been used or to put them to one side.
- Extend the activity to 4-digit numbers.

Name: ....

6a

Comparing and ordering numbers

Write the number each arrow points to.

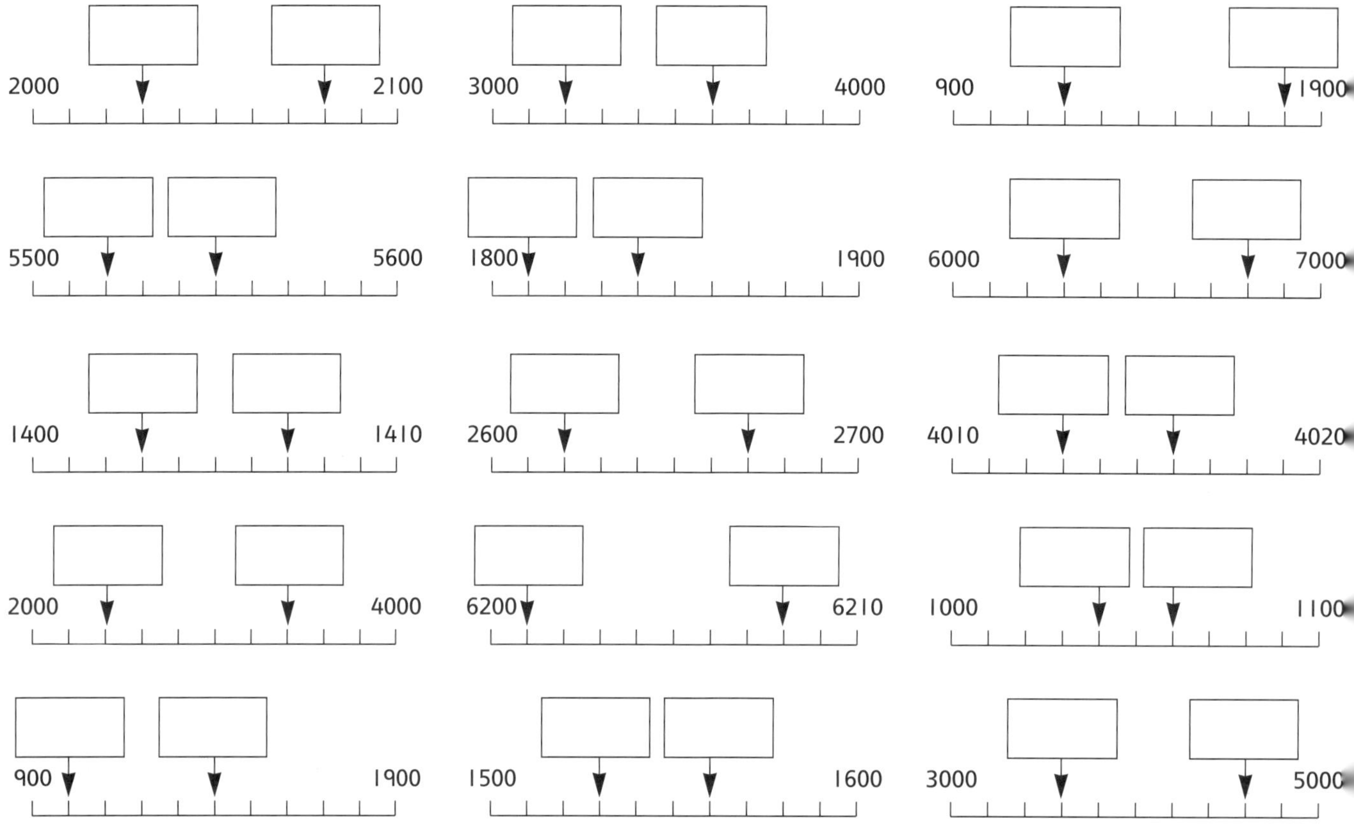

Write these sets of numbers in order in your books, starting with the smallest.

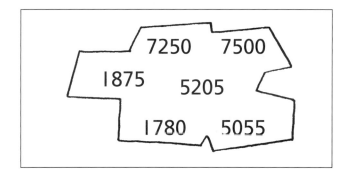

7250 7500
1875 5205
1780 5055

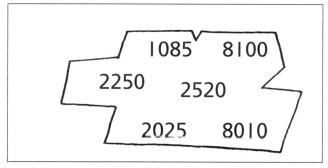

1085 8100
2250 2520
2025 8010

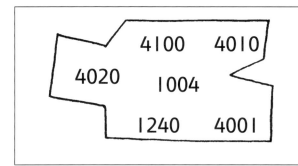

4100 4010
4020 1004
1240 4001

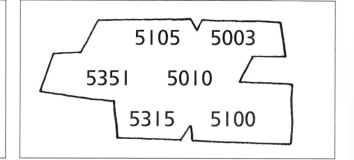

5105 5003
5351 5010
5315 5100

Name: ....

6b

Comparing and ordering numbers

3	9	4	6

How many 4-digit numbers can you make from these?
Write them all in order, starting with the smallest.

Now write your own four digits.

Ask a partner to write all the 4-digit numbers in order.

Name: ....

6c

Comparing and ordering numbers

Write all the numbers which fit each clue.

Which numbers are greater than 255 but less than 264?

Which numbers are smaller than 1000 but greater than 985?

Which numbers come between 794 and 805?

Which numbers are greater than 1150 and smaller than 1160?

Now make up some clues for your partner to answer.

LESSON 7 Estimation and approximation

Lesson objective

- to read and write the vocabulary of estimation and approximation, and make and justify estimates

Language

- estimate, rough, approximate

Resources

- counting stick, individual fan numbers or digit cards (Resource sheets 1 and 2), class number line, **PCM7a, 7b, 7c**

Prior learning

- estimating up to 100 objects

Teaching

whole class: about 15 minutes

- Explain to the children that this lesson is about estimating numbers.
- ***What does 'estimate' mean?***

  Discuss and establish that estimating gives a rough answer without counting, measuring or calculating accurately. And that it involves more than guessing – an estimate is based on something we know and is as accurate as possible.
- ***What does 'approximate' mean?***

  Discuss and establish that approximate answers are answers which are 'near enough'. We do not always need an exact number and often approximate to the nearest simple number. For example, a newspaper might say that there were 25 000 people at a football match. The organizers would know exactly how many tickets had been sold, but the exact number is not necessary. An approximate number is enough to give the readers an idea of the size of the crowd.
- Hold up the counting stick and explain that it represents the range of numbers from 0 to 100. Ask the children to count aloud in tens as you indicate the position of each 10 on the stick. Then ask individual children to point to the position of particular numbers which you say, such as 35, 82 and 49, and explain how they decided where each number lay.
- Point to different positions between the tenths marks on the stick and ask the children to show you an estimate of that number using their fan numbers or digit cards. Comment on the responses to reinforce the concept that you are not looking for exact answers and that reasonable estimates are all that is required.

Activities

about 20 minutes

Core (for whole class or average attainers)

Tell the children that they will be estimating numbers indicated on blank number lines. Give them **PCM7a**, making sure the children realize that each number line represents a different range of numbers. Draw the children's attention to the picture of the full jar of 1000 sweets in the second part of the activity. Point out that they will be estimating the approximate number of sweets in the other jars. Compare all the results. Was there much variation?

Extension (for extension lesson or higher attainers)

Work with this group for a few minutes using a counting stick, first with a range of 0 to 500, and then 100 to 200. Ask them to estimate the different positions on the line. Explain that they will be doing similar work on **PCM7b**. Emphasize that the number lines do not always start from 0, and that it is possible for individuals to have different answers for some of the positions.

Support (for reinforcement lesson or lower attainers)

Tell the children that they will be estimating and marking the position of particular numbers on a number line. Hand out **PCM7c**. Explain that they can use the class number line to help them, if they wish. It will also be helpful for the children to talk to each other about this work, sharing ideas and explaining to each other how they made their estimates.

Plenary

whole class: about 5 minutes

Ask the children who completed **PCM7a** to explain how they made their estimates of the numbers on the number lines, and invite comments from the other children. Initiate a discussion about any differing results.

Further activities

- Give each child a strip of card marked in ten equal sections on one side and blank on the other. Wrap an elastic band round it to slide along the strip. Ask some questions that involve estimating a position on the number strip, for example:
  If one end is 0 and the other end is 100, show me the approximate position of 30, 75, 68, 55, 12, and so on.

  Continue this activity using both the blank side for very approximate positions and the side marked in ten sections for greater accuracy. Change the range of the line and repeat for appropriate numbers.

Name: ....

Estimation and approximation

Estimate the numbers shown by these arrows.

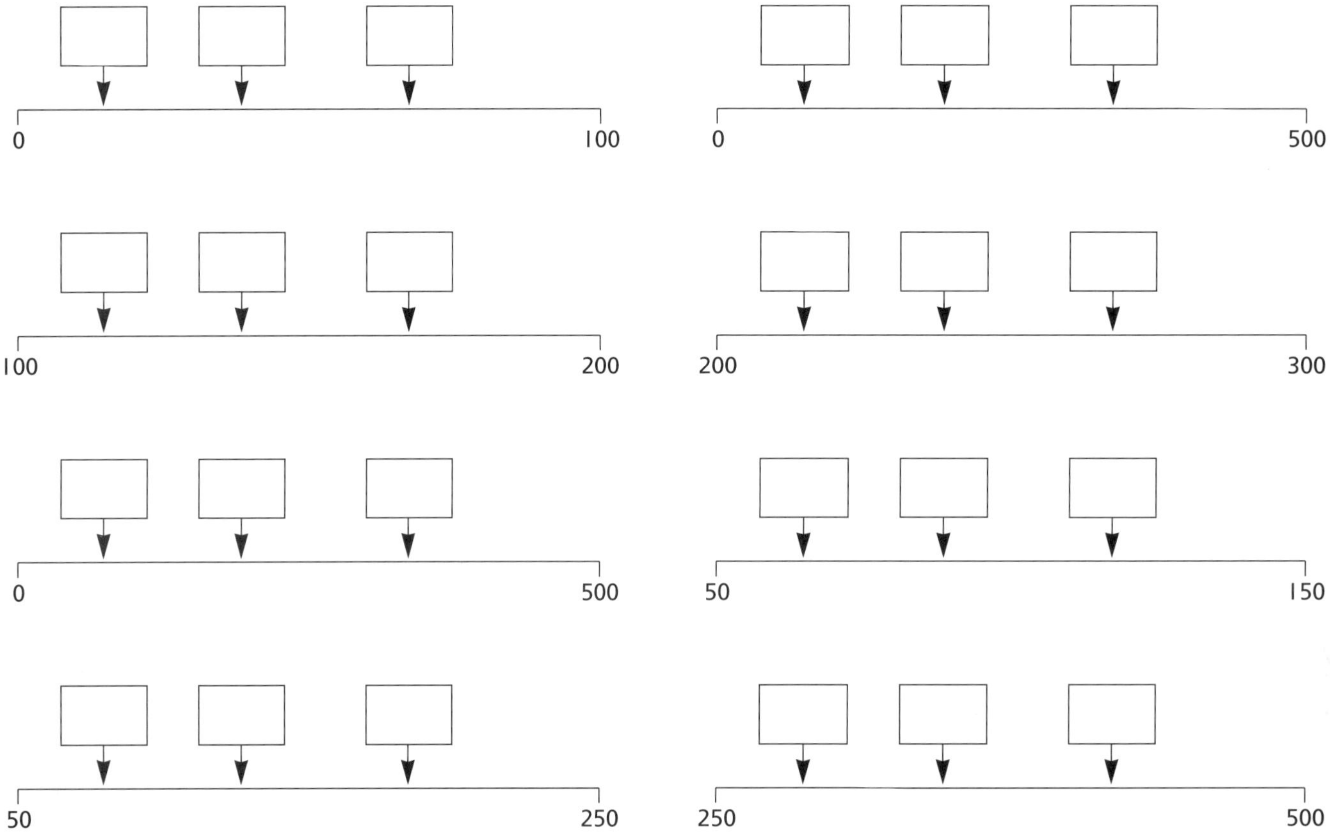

This jar holds 1000 sweets when it is full. Estimate the approximate number of sweets in each of these jars.

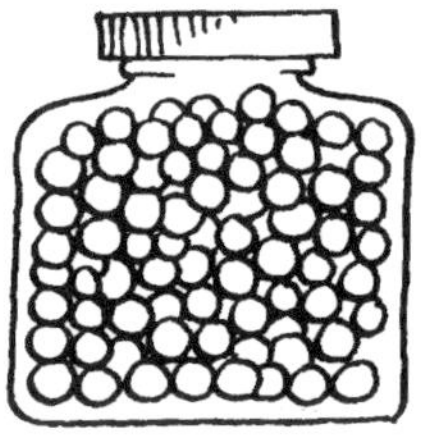

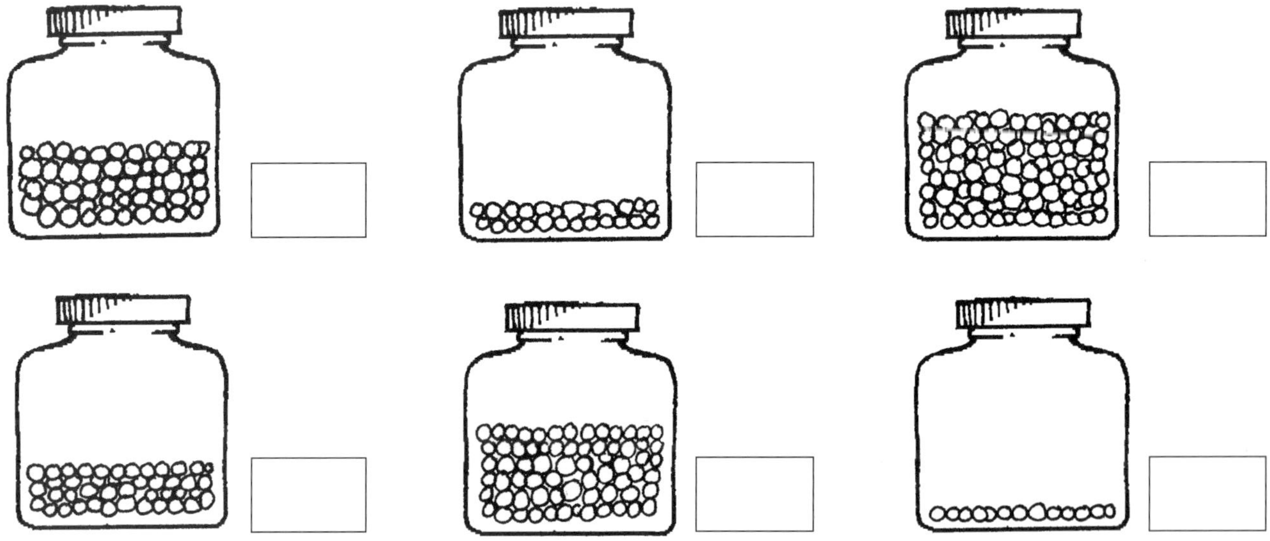

Name: ....

7b

Estimation and approximation

Estimate the numbers shown by the arrows on these number lines.

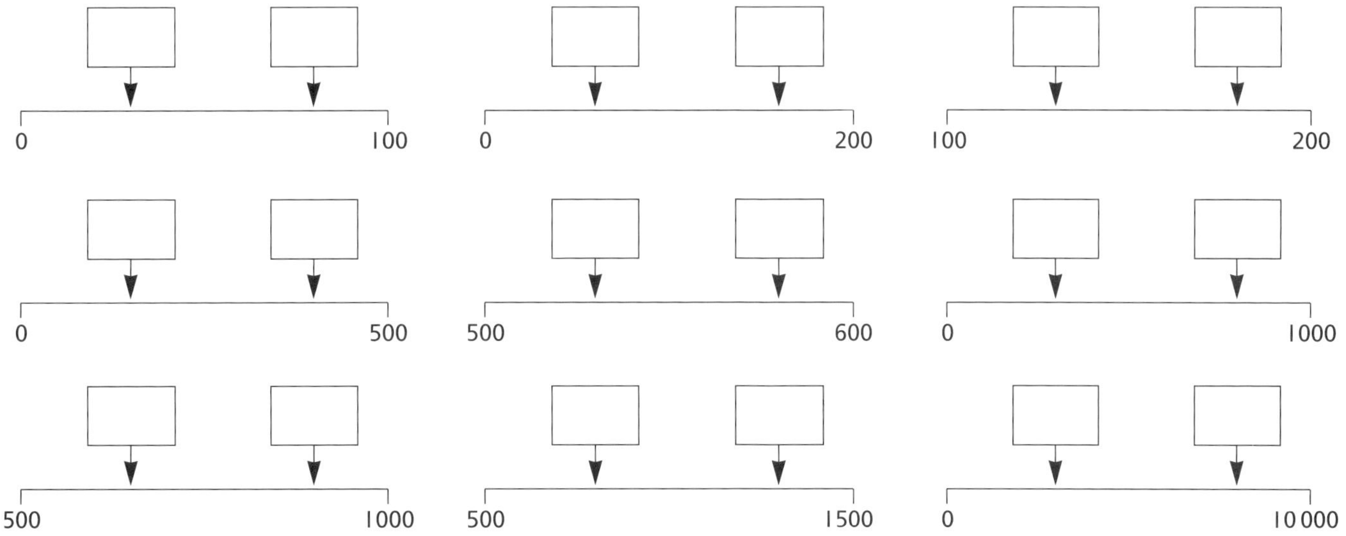

Estimate the position of these numbers on this number line.

752 126 317 945 63 608

Name: ....

7c

Estimation and approximation

Write these sets of numbers on the number lines.
Draw an arrow to show the approximate position of the extra number.

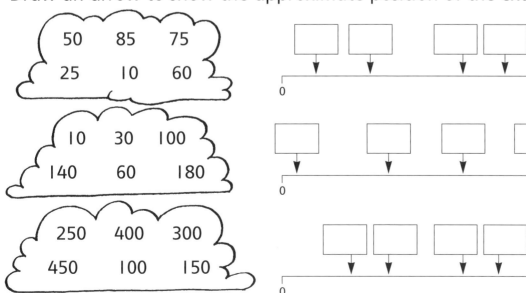

50 85 75
25 10 60

10 30 100
140 60 180

250 400 300
450 100 150

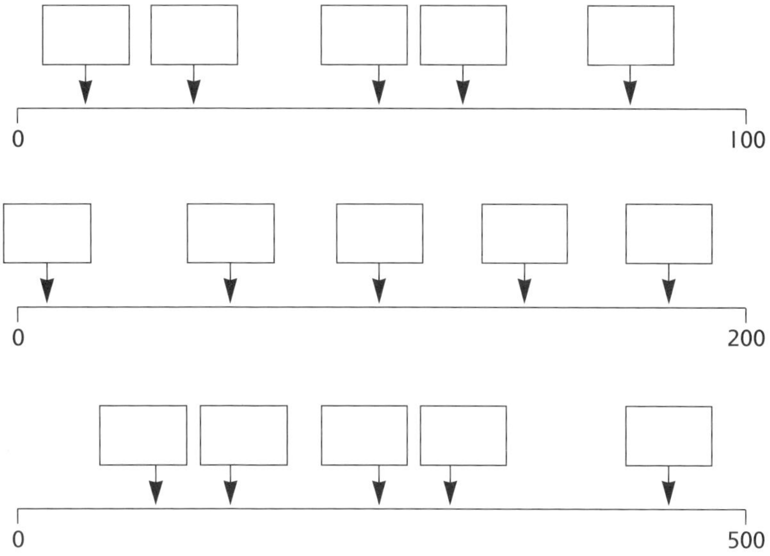

LESSON 8 Rounding numbers

Lesson objective

- to round any positive integer less than 1000 to the nearest 10 or 100

Language

- round, rounded, nearest, approximate

Resources

- class number line, digit cards with an extra 0 (Resource sheet 2), **PCM8a, 8b, 8c**

Prior learning

- rounding numbers to the nearest 10 or 100

Teaching

whole class: about 15 minutes

- Explain to the children that this lesson is about rounding numbers to the nearest 10 or 100, and learning how to use rounding to give approximate answers to calculations.
- ***What is 68 rounded to the nearest 10? What is 342 rounded to the nearest 10? What is 342 rounded to the nearest 100? Can anyone remember the rule we use to tell us whether to round a number up or down?***

  Establish that when rounding to the nearest 10, the units digit is considered, and that the tens digit is considered when rounding to the nearest 100. If the digit is less than 5, the number is rounded down. If the digit is 5 or greater, the number is rounded up.
- Ask the class to use their digit cards to show particular numbers which you say, rounded to the nearest 10 or the nearest 100.

  Round 34, 58, 85, 112 and 284 to the nearest 10.

  Round 109, 161, 243, 550 and 739 to the nearest 100.

  Round 745 to the nearest 10. Now round 745 to the nearest 100.
- Write 9×45 on the board. Tell the children that you want an approximate answer to this calculation, and not an exact answer.

  Can anyone think of an easy way to work out the approximate answer to this calculation?

  Establish by discussion that rounding 9 to 10 then multiplying 45 by 10 is an easy way to approximate.

  Is 450 greater or fewer than the exact answer? How do you know? What about 93 – 28? Can you think of an easy way to approximate the answer? Is 60 greater or less than the exact answer? How do you know?

  Repeat this activity for a few more approximate answers to calculations which cannot easily be done mentally.

Activities

about 15 minutes

Core (for whole class or average attainers)

Tell the children that they will be rounding numbers to the nearest 10 and 100 before answering some questions about approximate answers to calculations. Give them **PCM8a** and explain that the numbers in the first section are to be rounded both to the nearest 10 and the nearest 100. Explain that in the second section they should look at each calculation, choose one of the calculations in the box next to it which is the best approximation and write the answer to that calculation.

Extension (for extension lesson or higher attainers)

Give the children **PCM8b**. Explain that they will be finding easy ways to approximate some calculations, recording the method they used. In each case, they should indicate whether their approximation is greater than or less than the actual answer. Work through the first example with them, rounding the calculation to *160 + 140*. Write the approximate answer of 300, which is higher than the actual answer. Ask the children how they know this. Once you are sure they understand that they should round to the nearest 10, let them complete the **PCM**. Explain that it is possible for individuals to choose different rounding methods.

Support (for reinforcement lesson or lower attainers)

Provide the children with **PCM8c**. Tell them that they will be rounding numbers to the nearest 10 or 100 according to the instructions on the **PCM**. Read through the instructions with the group to make sure they are clear before they begin.

Plenary

whole class: about 10 minutes

Ask one of the children who did the 'Extension' activity to explain to the class what they did. Ask the other members of that group whether they used the same method and, if not, to explain theirs. Write *793 + 225* on the board and ask all the children to think of an easy way to approximate the answer. Repeat this for other calculations, reminding them that rounding is very useful in mental calculation.

Further activities

- Play 'Calculator rounding' in pairs. Player A inputs a calculation such as *493 + 568*, or *78 × 6* into their calculator. They ask Player B to give an answer to the calculation, rounded to the nearest 100. This is then checked with the calculator, with a point given for a correct answer. Take turns at this, with the first to, say, 10 points being the winner.
- To develop the activity, the answers can be rounded to the nearest 10.

Name: **8a**

Rounding numbers

Round these numbers to the nearest 10 and 100.

Number	nearest 10	nearest 100
127		
342		
265		
406		
555		
351		
746		
838		
684		

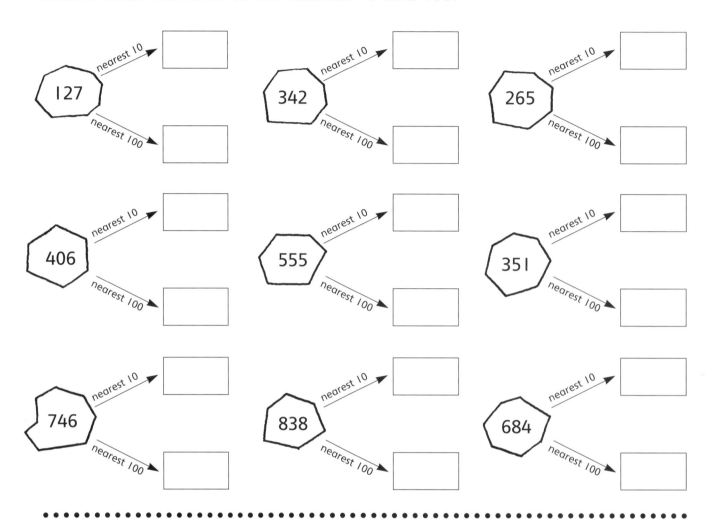

Circle the best way to round the following calculations.
Write the approximate answer.

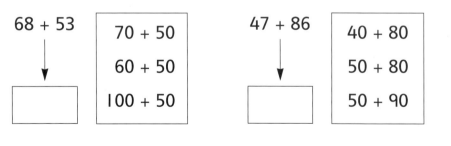

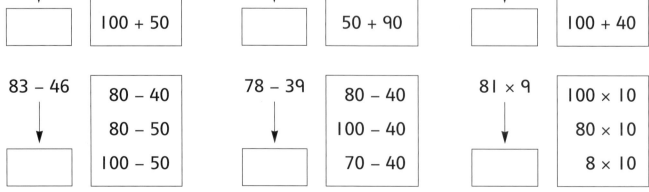

68 + 53	70 + 50 60 + 50 100 + 50
47 + 86	40 + 80 50 + 80 50 + 90
95 + 42	100 + 50 90 + 40 100 + 40
83 – 46	80 – 40 80 – 50 100 – 50
78 – 39	80 – 40 100 – 40 70 – 40
81 × 9	100 × 10 80 × 10 8 × 10

Name: ....

8b

Rounding numbers

Complete this table.

Calculation	Rounding	Approximate answer	Higher or lower than actual answer
157 + 139			
242 – 117			
309 + 114			
434 – 285			
615 + 178			
53 × 8			
93 × 9			
82 × 11			

Name: ....

8c

Rounding numbers

Round these numbers to the nearest 10. Draw a circle around your choice.

46: 40 / 60 / 50

52: 50 / 60 / 100

84: 80 / 90 / 40

65: 100 / 60 / 70

93: 90 / 100 / 95

Round these numbers to the nearest 100 and circle your choice.

128: 130 / 100 / 200

284: 300 / 200 / 290

355: 300 / 400 / 500

450: 500 / 400 / 600

349: 350 / 400 / 300

Round these numbers to the nearest 10.

183 → ☐ 256 → ☐ 385 → ☐ 107 → ☐

244 → ☐ 491 → ☐ 504 → ☐ 375 → ☐

LESSON 9 Negative numbers

Lesson objective

- to recognize negative numbers in context

Language

- positive, negative, minus, above zero, below zero

Resources

- thermometer, picture of a thermometer scale on the board, class number line (extending beyond 0 to at least –10), individual digit cards including a card with a minus sign (Resource sheet 2), **PCM 9a, 9b, 9c**

Prior learning

- adding and subtracting with the use of a number line
- using a thermometer to record the temperature in weather studies, ideally in winter when negative temperatures have been recorded

Teaching

whole class: about 20 minutes

- Explain to the children that this lesson is about recognizing negative numbers.
- Talk to the class about temperature records. With reference to the thermometer and the picture on the board, ask questions such as the following and indicate the readings on the picture:

  What is the temperature today? What would it be if it was 2 degrees warmer? What would it be if it was 2 degrees colder?

  Establish that the higher temperature would be indicated up the scale and the lower one down the scale.

  What happens to the temperature when the weather is very cold? What do we call the temperature when it falls to 1 degree below zero? What about 3 degrees below zero?

  Explain that when the temperature falls to zero, it is just cold enough for water to start to turn to ice, so puddles can become icy. It can get colder than this.

  Establish that such readings are called 'minus 1' and 'minus 3', and recorded using a minus sign before the number. Explain that 'minus 3' is often called 'negative 3' in mathematics because the numbers less than zero are negative numbers. Indicate the negative numbers on the thermometer and on the picture. Point to different readings on the thermometer picture, both positive and negative, and ask the children to give the temperatures.

  What is the lowest temperature on the scale? What is the highest temperature? Which temperature is lower: –3°C or –5°C? Which is higher: –1°C or 1°C?

- Refer now to the number line. Explain that it shows numbers above and below 0, those above being called *positive numbers* – the numbers we normally count with – and those below being called *negative numbers*. Ask the children to start at 0 and count forwards to 10; then start at 0 and count backwards to negative 10. Ask them to start at –10 and count forwards to 10, then back to –10. Talk about the place of 0 and establish that it comes between 1 and –1.
- Ask the children to use their digit cards to show answers to questions such as the following:

  What comes after –2? What comes before 1? What is 1 more than –5? What is 1 less than –6? What is 1 more than –1?

  And so on.

Activities

about 15 minutes

Core (for whole class or average attainers)

Give the children **PCM9a**, explaining that they will be filling in missing numbers on number lines and continuing number line patterns. Both these activities include using negative numbers.

Extension (for extension lesson or higher attainers)

Explain to the children that they will be completing number sequences which involve some negative numbers. Hand out **PCM9b**, pointing out that they are asked to write the rule for each sequence. The children then make up some sequences for themselves.

Support (for reinforcement lesson or lower attainers)

Repeat some of the counting activities done earlier with the class involving counting on and back through zero. Tell the children that they are going to write down the temperature shown on five thermometers before completing two number lines. Give them **PCM9c** and stay with the group for a few minutes to make sure the children understand the activity.

Plenary

whole class: about 5 minutes

Draw a blank number line on the board and write the range below it, for example –5 and 5. Ask individual children to point to particular numbers you say on the line. Then point to numbers on the number line and ask the class to show you those numbers using their digit cards.

Further activities

- Use a newspaper or carry out a search on the Internet for the daily temperatures of some very cold places. If possible, keep a daily record for a week of the temperature in one of these places, comparing the daily increase or decrease in temperature and comparing it with the temperature in the UK.

Name: ....

9a

Negative numbers

Write the missing numbers on these number lines.

☐ −4 ☐ ☐ −1 0 1 2 ☐ ☐ ☐

−9 ☐ ☐ ☐ −5 ☐ −3 ☐ ☐ 0 1 ☐ ☐ ☐ 5

☐ ☐ −7 ☐ ☐ ☐ ☐ −2 −1 ☐ ☐ ☐ 3 4 ☐ ☐ 7 8

Continue the patterns on these number lines.
Write the numbers that the penguin lands on.

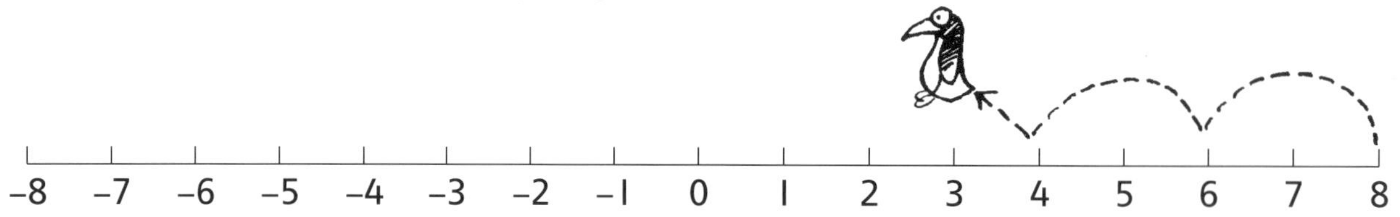

8 6 4

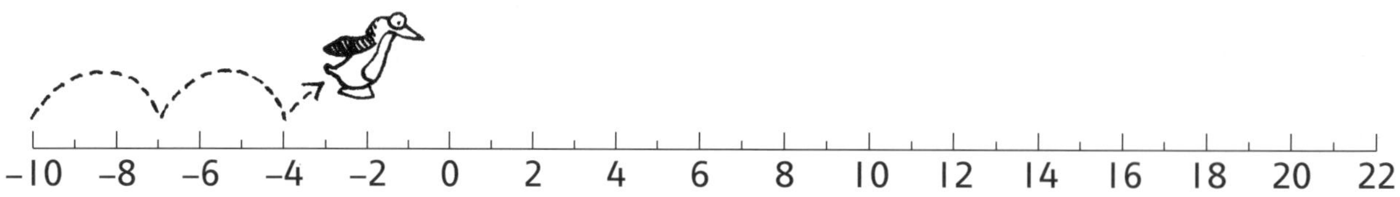

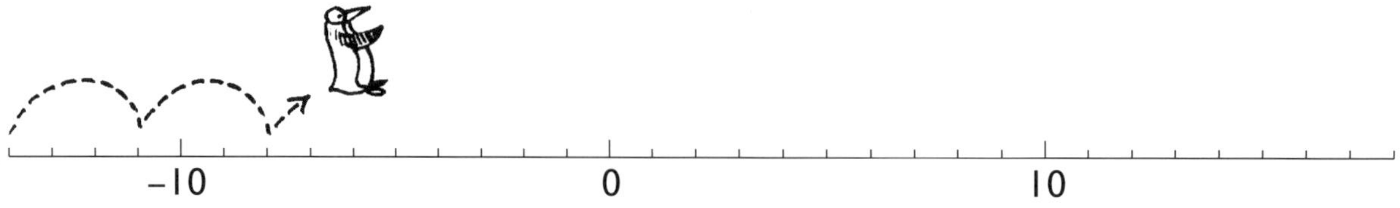

Name: ....

9b

Negative numbers

Copy and complete these number sequences.
Write the rule for each sequence in your book.

1.	–6	–4					6	8
2.				–3	0		6	9
3.	–7			–1		3	5	
4.			–4		4	8		16
5.	–10			–1		5	8	

Now make up five more negative number sequences and write them in your book.

Name: ....

9c

Negative numbers

Write the temperatures shown on these thermometers.

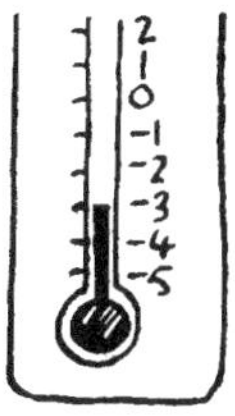

☐ °C

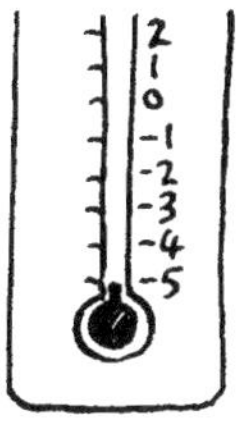

☐ °C

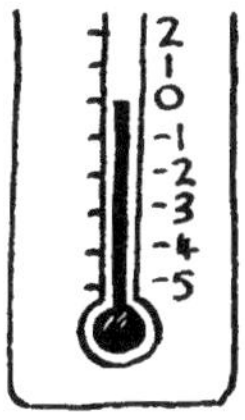

☐ °C

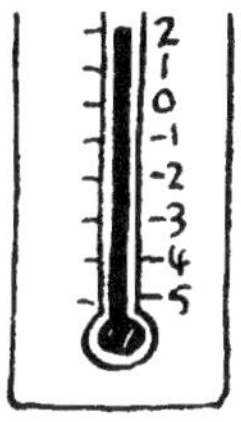

☐ °C

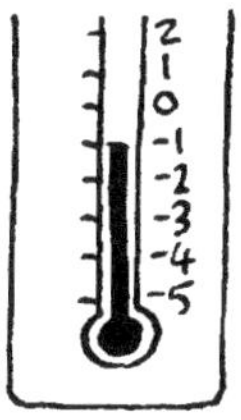

☐ °C

Write the missing numbers on these number lines.

–8						–2	–1	0	1			4			

				–4		0	2	4		8					

LESSON 10 Number sequences

Lesson objective

- to recognize and extend number sequences formed by counting on and back in steps of constant size, extending beyond 0 when counting back

Language

- sequence, predict, continue, rule

Resources

- the following number sequences written on the board:

Set 1:	Set 2:
4, 7, 10, 13, __	__, 16, 20, __, 28, 32, __, __
37, 32, 27, 22, __	13, __, 19, 22, __, __, 31, __
15, 18, 21, 24, __	26, 21, __, 11, 6, __, –4, __
16, 12, 8, 4, __	__, __, 42, 39, 36, __, __, 27

number grids (Resource Sheet 4), class 1–100 square (Resource Sheet 3), counters, **PCM10a, 10b, 10c**

Prior learning

- counting on and back in steps of different sizes from different starting points
- recognizing negative numbers on a number line

Teaching

whole class: about 20 minutes

- Explain to the children that this lesson is about recognizing and extending sequences of numbers.
- Ask the class to count on in fives from 0 to 50, then back to –10.

  What did you notice about the units digits in that sequence?

  Ask the class to count on in fives from 1 to 51 and back to 1.

  What did you notice about the units digits in that sequence?

  Ask the class to count on in tens from 0 to 50 and back to –50.

  Is there a pattern in the units digits in that sequence?

  Ask the class to count on in twenty-fives from 0 to 200 and back to 0.

  Is there a pattern? Can you count back from 0 into negative numbers?
- Explain that you are going to count to the class in regular steps and they have to work out what the step is:

  8, 11, 14, 17, 20, 23 …

  Now choose a different step and count backwards. Can the children work out the step you are using? Can they continue the sequence? Can they extend it beyond 0?

  Tell the children that these are number sequences, that is, a series of numbers which follow in steps according to a particular rule.
- Ask one child to provide their own sequence by counting on or back in any small step from any number.

  What is the rule for that sequence?

  Repeat this activity with different children.
- Look at the first sequence in Set 1 on the board.

  What is the next number in the sequence? How do you know?

  Explain that the rule for this sequence is 'add 3' because each number in the sequence is 3 more than the previous number.

  What is the next number in the sequence? And the next?
- Look at the second sequence in Set 1 on the board.

  What is the next number in the sequence? What is the rule for this sequence?
  What is the next number in the sequence? And the next?

  Repeat this for the next two sequences.

- Look at the first sequence in Set 2 on the board. Explain that some of the numbers in this sequence are missing.

  Can anyone work out the rule for this sequence? How did you work it out? What are the missing numbers?

  Repeat this for the other three sequences.

Activities

about 15 minutes

Core (for whole class or average attainers)

Give the children **PCM10a**. Tell them that they will be continuing number sequences and explaining the rules before making up some sequences of their own, according to given rules. They finish by filling in the missing numbers in some sequences.

Extension (for extension lesson or higher attainers)

Point out that the children will be recording different counts on six number grids and using the patterns they find to make predictions. Give them **PCM10b** and make sure they understand the instructions before they begin.

Support (for reinforcement lesson or lower attainers)

Work with this group. Give each child the 1–100 square and about 20 counters. Count together in steps of 3 or 4 from a particular number and ask the children to place a counter on each number in the sequence. Record the sequence of numbers covered by the counters on **PCM10c**. Do this twice more, starting from different numbers. Then tell them that they can use the 1–100 square to help them to complete the sequences for the second part of the activity on the **PCM**.

Plenary

whole class: about 5 minutes

Ask one child to make up a rule for a number sequence, for example + 5. Ask another to give a starting number. Ask the class to say the sequence together. Repeat this with different starting numbers. Explain to the class that they have been learning to extend number sequences by recognizing their rules, which will be very useful for some investigative activities they will do in the future.

Further activities

- Play 'Stick sequences' where the children make a pattern of squares from sticks. They then investigate the number of sticks used for each of the squares

Number of squares	Number of sticks
1	4
2	7
3	10

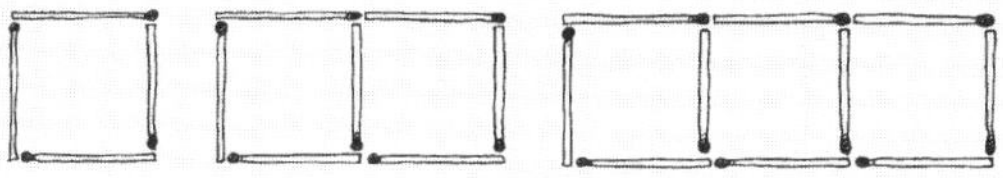

  Encourage them to look at the patterns generated and to predict the next numbers in the sequence.
- Develop the activity by making triangles from the sticks.

Name: ....

Number sequences

Continue these sequences and write the rule for each one.

29	33	37								Rule
42	47	52								Rule
83	80	77								Rule
68	62	56								Rule
17	26	35								Rule

Make up your own sequences with these rules.

Rule: add 6										
Rule: subtract 4										

Now write the missing numbers.

	27			39	43		
	9	7			1		
				54		44	39
	44		56	62			

Name: ....

10b

Number sequences

You will need: Number Grid 1

- Count on in fours from 0, colouring in the numbers, so it begins 3, 7…

  What pattern do you notice?

- Count on in fours on the other five grids.

  What patterns do you notice?

- Use different colours to show counting on in threes and fives on all six grids.

- Describe your patterns.

Name: ....

10c

Number sequences

Record your sequences here.

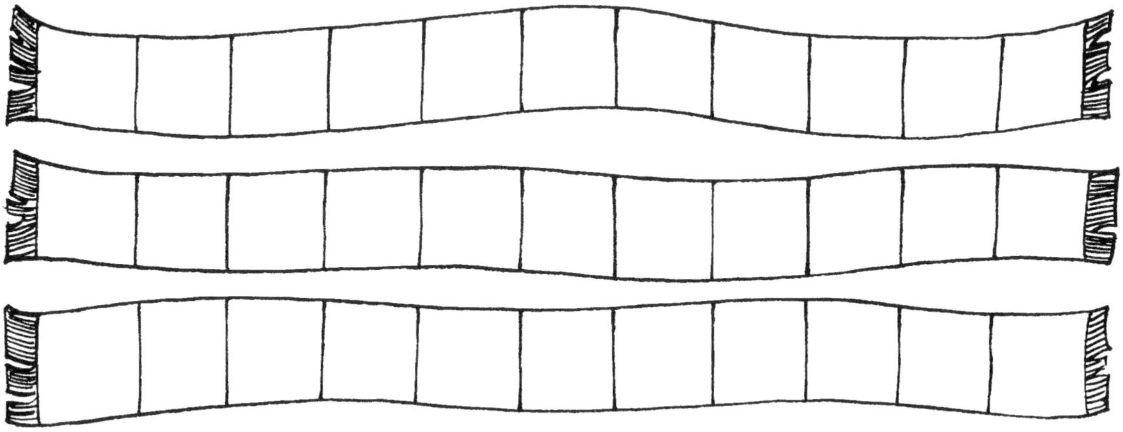

Now complete these sequences.

37 40 43 ____ ____ ____ ____ ____ ____ ____

22 27 32 ____ ____ ____ ____ ____ ____ ____

LESSON 11 Odds and evens

Lesson objective

- to recognize odd and even numbers up to 1000 and some of their properties, including the outcomes of sums and differences of pairs of odd/even numbers

Language

- odd, even, sequence, digit, consecutive

Resources

- a set of 10 random numbers to 100 on the board (both odd and even), individual fan numbers or digit cards (Resource sheets 1 and 2), **PCM11a, 11b, 11c**

Prior learning

- recognizing odd and even numbers to at least 100
- recognizing sequences

Teaching *whole class: about 15 minutes*

- Explain to the children that this lesson is about learning more rules about odd and even numbers. Remind them that they already know some rules for recognizing odd and even numbers.
- Look at the set of numbers on the board. Ask a volunteer to pick an even number from the set. Ask another to pick an odd number. Repeat for a few more odd and even numbers.

  What is the rule for finding an even number?

  Even numbers divide exactly by 2 and they have a units digit of 0, 2, 4, 6 or 8.

  What is the rule for finding an odd number?

  Odd numbers have 1 left over when divided by 2 and they have a units digit of 1, 3, 5, 7 or 9. Explain that both of these rules are true for any number, even very large numbers.
- Ask the children to use their fan numbers or digit cards to show:

  An odd number. An even number. An odd number greater than 50. An even number greater than 100. An even number between 251 and 257. An odd number between 500 and 520. What is the next even number after 456? What is the odd number before 201? What is the even number after 398?
- Ask the children to give you the sequence of the first five even numbers (from 0 to 10) and record it on the board. Explain that these are consecutive even numbers because each number in the sequence is the next even number and there are no other even numbers which could come between.

  What is the difference between each consecutive even number?

  Repeat the activity for the sequence of the first five odd numbers (from 0 to 10).

Activities *about 20 minutes*

Core (for whole class or average attainers)

Give the children **PCM11a** and explain that they will be working with number sequences involving odd and even numbers. They then look for rules for totals and differences of odd and even numbers.

Extension (for extension lesson or higher attainers)

Hand out **PCM11b** and tell the children that they will be investigating the totals of consecutive numbers to see if they are odd or even. Ask for examples of consecutive numbers and then read the questions. Ask how they might record their results.

Support (for reinforcement lesson or lower attainers)

Point out to the children they will be looking at the units digits in some numbers and using this to classify the numbers into 'odd' and 'even' sets. Ask the children what all odd numbers 'end in' (the units value). Do this orally, then give them **PCM11c** and ensure that the children record the units digits correctly in the box. Repeat this for the even numbers. Explain that they need to look at each number on the tree, decide whether it is odd or even, then record it in the appropriate set on the sheet.

Plenary ***whole class: about 5 minutes***

Ask the children to tell you all the rules they now know about odd and even numbers. Encourage the use of precise language and compile a list of the rules such as:

The units digit of an even number is 0, 2, 4, 6 or 8.

The units digit of an odd number is 1, 3, 5, 7 or 9.

The sum of any two even numbers is even.

The sum of any two odd numbers is even.

The sum of an odd number and an even number is odd.

The difference between two odd or two even numbers is even.

Write the rules on the board.

Further activities

- ***Are we an odd class or an even class?*** Investigate interesting numerical data which can be classified as odd or even, for example: the number of children in the class, house numbers, age in months, height in centimetres, number of children in the family, birthday month, and so on.
- Develop this activity by putting the information on a simple computer database to sort and interpret the data.

Name: ....

11a

Odds and evens

Write the missing numbers in these sequences.

153			159	161				
			218	220			226	
609	607				599			
		352		348	346			
786			792	794				

Use these to help you to complete the rules for adding and subtracting odd and even numbers.

15 + 10 = ______ 18 + 12 = ______

14 + 15 = ______ 11 + 19 = ______

17 + 17 = ______ 10 + 14 = ______

12 − 9 = ______ 16 − 12 = ______

20 − 16 = ______ 15 − 9 = ______

19 − 12 = ______ 17 − 13 = ______

Now write other calculations of your own to test the rules.

Even or Odd?

even + even = ☐

even + odd = ☐

odd + odd = ☐

even − odd = ☐

odd − odd = ☐

even − even = ☐

odd − even = ☐

Name: ....

11b

Odds and evens

You are going to investigate consecutive numbers.

- Do you get an odd or an even total when you add two consecutive numbers? Why?
- What about when you add three consecutive numbers?
- Or four consecutive numbers?

Record your results and explain any patterns you find in your book.

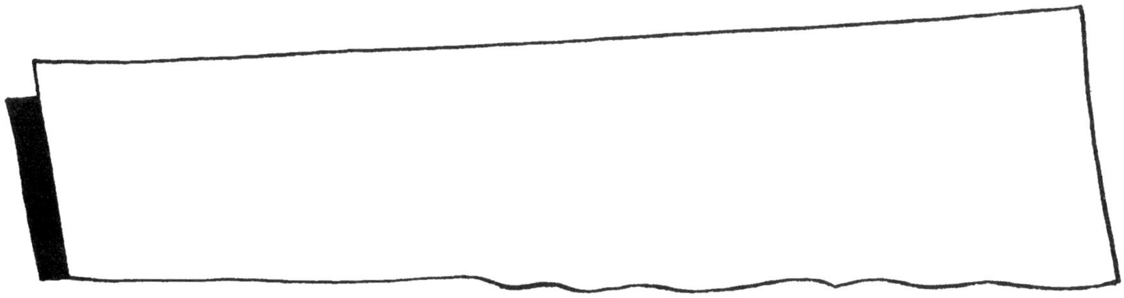

Name: ....

11c

Odds and evens

Write these numbers in the correct set.

Odd numbers	Even numbers
end in	end in

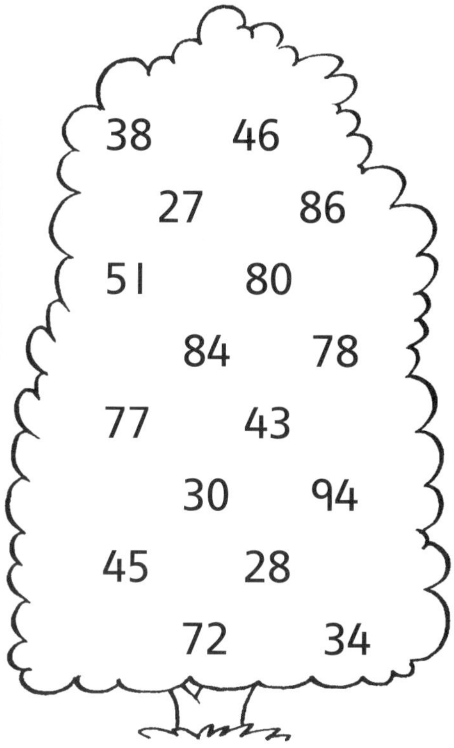

LESSON 12 Recognizing multiples

Lesson objective

- to recognize multiples of 2, 3, 4, 5 and 10, up to the tenth multiple

Language

- multiple, digit, divisible

Resources

- class 1–100 square (Resource sheet 3), a set of about ten numbers to 40 on the board (some of which are multiples of 3, the rest of them multiples of 4), **PCM12a, 12b, 12c**

Prior learning

- recognizing multiples of 2, 5, 10, 50 and 100
- understanding what the multiple of a number is

Teaching

whole class: about 15 minutes

- Explain to the children that this lesson is about recognizing multiples of particular numbers.
- ***What does 'multiple' mean?***

  Establish that a multiple of a number can be divided exactly by that number, so 9 is a multiple of 3 because it can be divided exactly by 3.

  Remind them that they can already recognize multiples of 2, 5, 10, 50 and 100.

  Give me a number which is a multiple of 10. How do we recognize a multiple of 10? Give me a number which is a multiple of 100. How do we recognize a multiple of 100? Give me a number which is a multiple of 5. How do we recognize a multiple of 5?

  Ask them to say the multiples of 2 up to 30. Point to the numbers on the 1–100 square as they do so.

  How do we recognize a multiple of 2?
- Ask the class to count in steps of 4 to 40, starting at 4.

  Of which number are all those numbers multiples?

  Point out the relationship with the multiples of 2. Ask if 24 is a multiple of 4. Give some more examples, including some which are not multiples of 4.
- Ask the children to count in steps of 3 to 30, starting at 3.

  Of which number are all those numbers multiples?

  Ask if 18 is a multiple of 3. Is 20? Explain that a very useful rule for knowing if a number is a multiple of 3 is to add the digits to see if the sum is divisible by 3. So for the number 18, the sum of the digits is 9, which is divisible by 3. So the number 18 is a multiple of 3.

  20 is not a multiple of 8 because the digits add up to 2, and 2 cannot be divided by 3.
- Look at the set of numbers on the board. Ask a volunteer to select a multiple of 3 and circle it, then ask another to select a multiple of 4 and underline it. Repeat this with different children until all the numbers have been used. Leave this visible on the board to help the children with the activities.

Activities

about 20 minutes

Core (for whole class or average attainers)

Tell the children that they will be recording numbers on a tree diagram. Give them **PCM12a** and explain how the decision tree works. Choose any number from the top of the sheet and work through the questions on the tree until the number reaches the end of a branch. When you are confident that the children understand what to do, ask them to do the same for all the other numbers.

Extension (for extension lesson or higher attainers)

Point out to the children that they will be trying to find the 'odd number out' in sets of numbers with the same multiple. Give them **PCM12b**, making sure they understand that they need to write the reason why they chose each particular odd number out.

Support (for reinforcement lesson or lower attainers)

Explain to the group that they are going to indicate the multiples of 2, 3 and 4 on the 1–100 square on **PCM12c**. Towards the end of the lesson go back to this group and ask about the patterns they notice on the 1–100 square.

Plenary

whole class: about 5 minutes

Ask the children who completed **PCM12c** to explain what they have found out to the rest of the class. Ask other children to suggest a number less than 100 which is a multiple of 3 for the 'Support' group to check.

Further activities

- Play 'What's my number?' Each child needs a set of fan numbers to make any 2-digit number. The teacher also makes a number, but hides it from the rest of the class. The class then asks questions with a 'Yes' or 'No' answer, such as:
  Is the number greater than 50?
  Is it a multiple of 3?
  The children check their number and change it, if necessary, in an attempt to match the teacher's number. Further clues are given until all the children have matched the teacher's number. It is helpful to write the questions on the board so that the children can check their number more easily.

Name: ....

12a

Recognizing multiples

Look at this multiple tree diagram.
Put each number through it to see where it ends up.

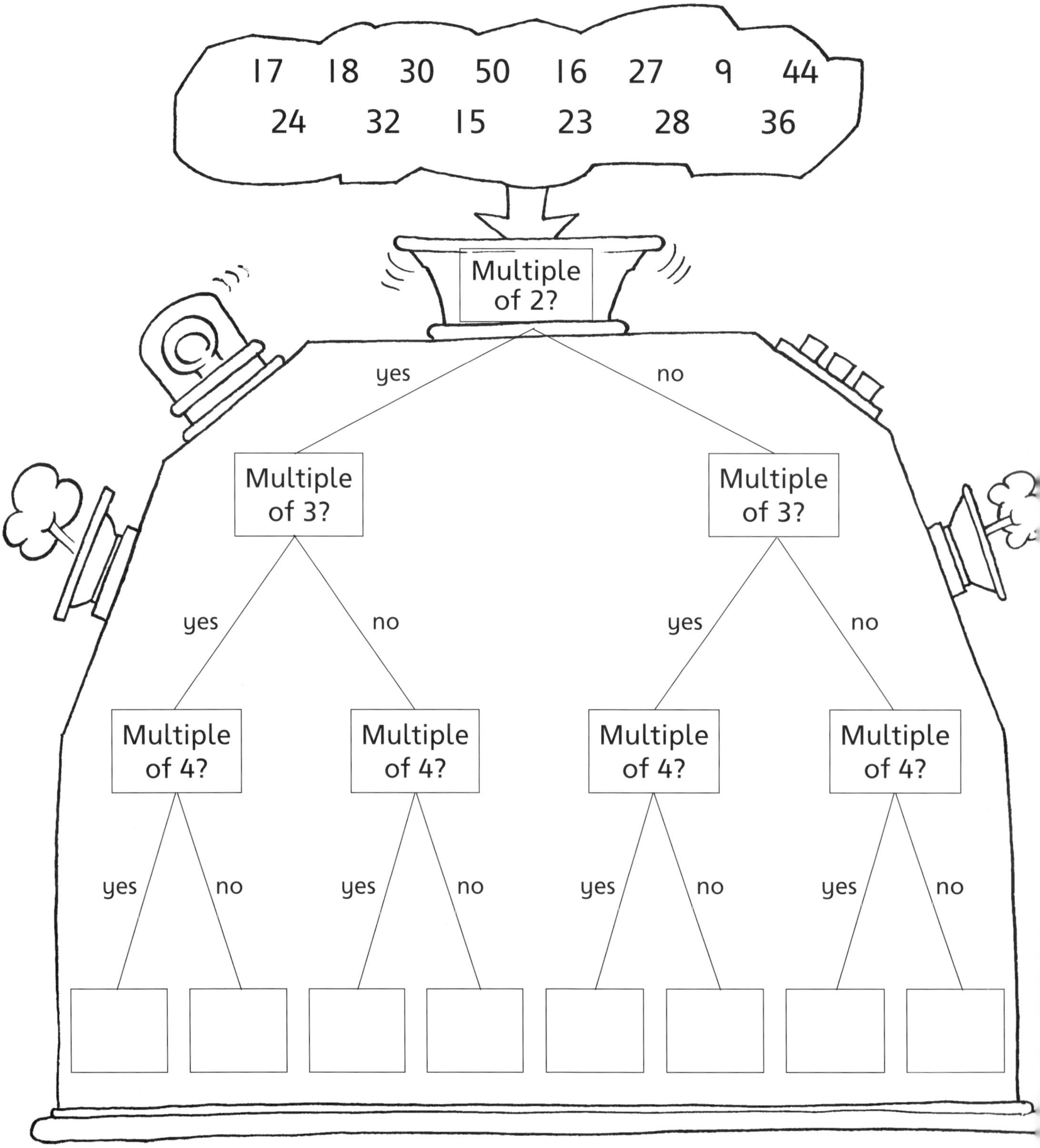

Put more numbers of your own through the machine.
Why are two boxes still empty?

Name: ....

12b

Recognizing multiples

Circle the odd one out in each set.
Write why each number is the odd one out.

38	84	46	70	83	92	______________
53	60	69	72	87	45	______________
45	70	100	90	120	60	______________
80	92	96	64	54	76	______________
800	400	700	200	550	900	______________
75	95	80	35	40	64	______________
138	108	114	180	160	153	______________
150	300	500	605	100	450	______________

Name: ....

12c

Recognizing multiples

In the 1–100 square:

- Colour the multiples of 2 yellow.
- Circle the multiples of 3 in blue.
- Cross out the multiples of 4.

What patterns do you notice?

1	2	3	4	5	6	7	8	9	10
11	12	13	14	15	16	17	18	19	20
21	22	23	24	25	26	27	28	29	30
31	32	33	34	35	36	37	38	39	40
41	42	43	44	45	46	47	48	49	50
51	52	53	54	55	56	57	58	59	60
61	62	63	64	65	66	67	68	69	70
71	72	73	74	75	76	77	78	79	80
81	82	83	84	85	86	87	88	89	90
91	92	93	94	95	96	97	98	99	100

LESSON 13 Non-unitary fractions

Lesson objective

- to recognize simple fractions that are several parts of a whole, such as $\frac{2}{3}$ or $\frac{5}{8}$

Language

- fraction, names for fractions

Resources

- a large circle drawn on the board divided into 8 equal parts, a rectangle drawn on the board showing 5 equal parts, cubes, **PCM13a, 13b, 13c**

Prior learning

- recognizing and writing unit fractions and beginning to recognize fractions that are several parts of a whole

Teaching

whole class: about 20 minutes

- Explain to the children that this lesson is about fractions. Remind them that they already know some fractions. Ask:

  What is a fraction?

  and establish that a fraction is part of something. Revise the previous work on fractions by asking questions such as the following, and recording the notation for the answers on the board. Each time, point out that the number of equal parts is the bottom number of the fraction:

  If an orange has been divided into two equal parts, what fraction of the whole orange is each part?

  If a bar of chocolate has been divided into three equal parts, what fraction of the whole bar is each part?

  If a square has been divided into four equal parts, what fraction of the whole square is each part?

  If a cake has been divided into ten equal parts, what fraction of the whole cake is each part?

  If I had three pieces of the cake, what fraction of the cake would I have?

  If I had 20 sweets and I gave you one quarter of them, how many sweets would you have? What fraction of the sweets would I have left? What if I gave you ten sweets?

  If necessary, draw these as a diagram on the board.

- Tell the children that you are going to study some more fractions.

  Look at the circle on the board.

  How many equal parts has the circle been divided into? What do you think we call each fraction?

  Establish that each part is one eighth and write $\frac{1}{8}$ on each part of the circle. Outline three adjacent segments.

  What fraction of the circle is this?

  Record the answer as $\frac{3}{8}$ on the board.

  What fraction of the circle would 5 of these parts be?

  Record $\frac{5}{8}$ on the board.

  What about 6 parts? 7? 2?

- Look at the rectangle on the board.

  What fraction of the whole shape is each part?

  Record the answer as $\frac{1}{5}$ on the board

What fraction is 2 parts? 3? 4?

Record each in fraction notation on the board.

- Draw another circle on the board, this time with no divisions. Explain that you want to show $\frac{3}{4}$ on this circle and ask a child to demonstrate how they would do it. Encourage them to 'cut' the shape into 4 equal pieces and then shade 3 of the pieces. Draw a rectangle on the board and ask a child to show $\frac{4}{5}$ of the rectangle.

Activities

about 15 minutes

Core (for whole class or average attainers)

Give the children **PCM13a** and explain that they will be identifying and colouring fractions of different shapes.

Extension (for extension lesson or higher attainers)

Point out to the children that they will be making patterns on different grids by colouring $\frac{3}{4}$ of each grid. Provide **PCM13b** and encourage them to be creative and make each pattern different.

Support (for reinforcement lesson or lower attainers)

Give each child a copy of **PCM13c** and 6 cubes. Look at the top rectangle together and ask the children to place a cube on $\frac{1}{6}$ of the rectangle. Repeat this placing cubes on $\frac{2}{6}$, $\frac{3}{6}$, $\frac{4}{6}$, $\frac{5}{6}$, $\frac{6}{6}$ and $\frac{1}{2}$ of the rectangle. Explain that they will be colouring fractions of the other shapes according to the instructions on the sheet. Make sure they can read the fractions before they begin.

Plenary

whole class: about 5 minutes

Ask the group who were working on **PCM15b** to explain their activity to the rest of the children. Ask them how many squares on each grid were coloured:

So $\frac{3}{4}$ of 16 is? Can you work out $\frac{3}{4}$ of 12?

Ask the children who completed **PCM15a** to describe how they found the fractions of their shapes. For example, to show three quarters of a shape, ensure they 'cut' the shape into 4 equal pieces before colouring in 3 of the pieces.

Further activities

- Give each child a 6×4 piece of 2cm squared paper so that each child has 24 squares. Ask them to fold the grid to show you one half of the grid, one quarter of the grid, three quarters, one third, two thirds, and so on.
- Draw a large circle or rectangle on the board. Ask the children to draw a line on the shape to show the approximate position to cut it into $\frac{3}{4}$ and $\frac{1}{4}$. Use other fractions and vary the shapes, including irregular shapes to make the estimates more difficult.

Name: ....

Non-unitary fractions

Colour $\frac{3}{4}$ of each shape.

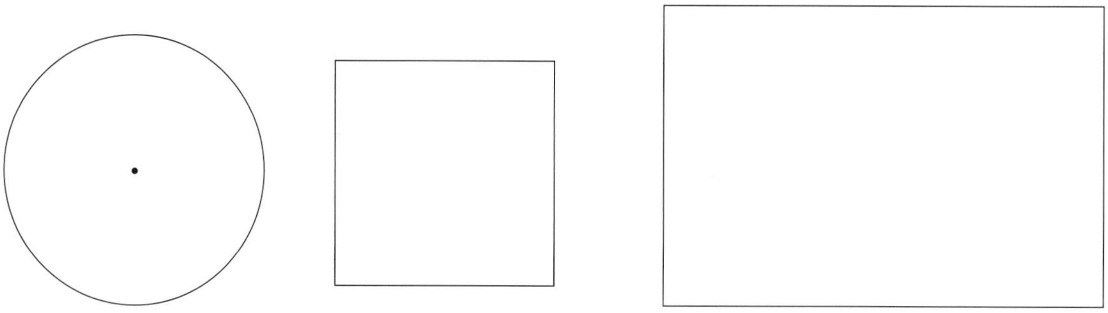

Colour $\frac{2}{3}$ of each shape.

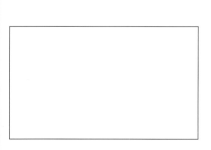

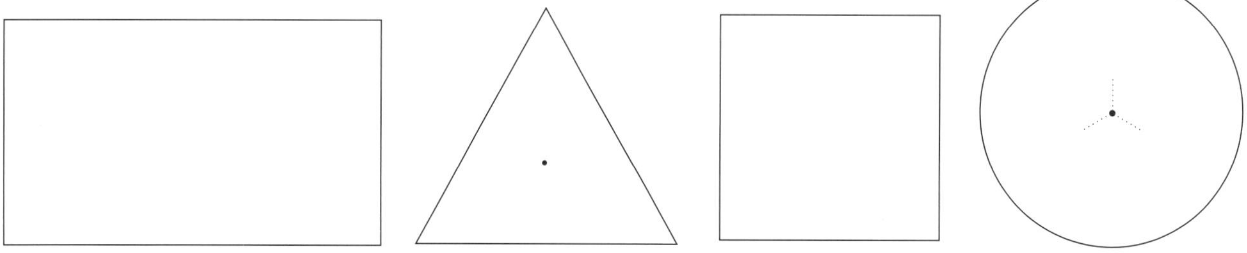

Colour $\frac{3}{5}$ of each shape.

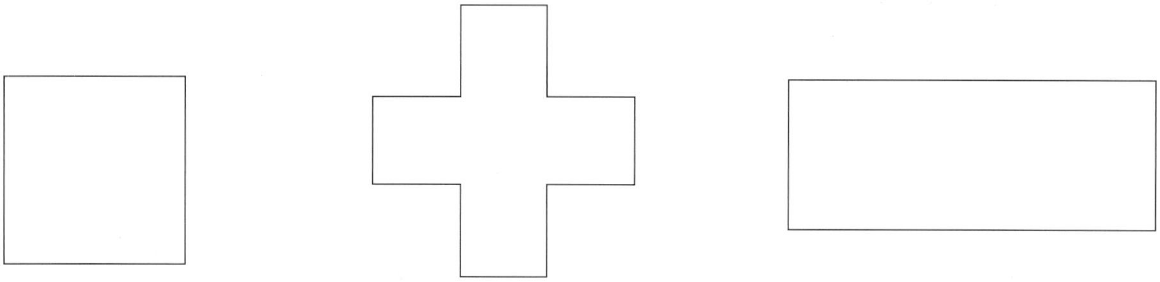

Colour $\frac{7}{8}$ of each shape.

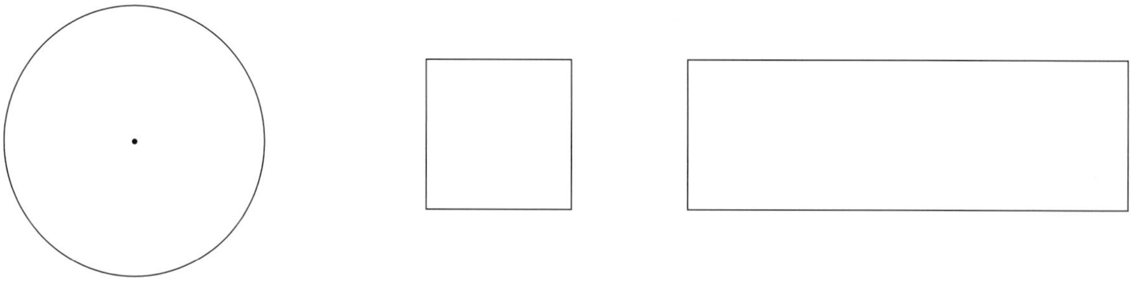

Name: ....

13b

Non-unitary fractions

Colour $\frac{3}{4}$ of each of these grids. Make each one different.

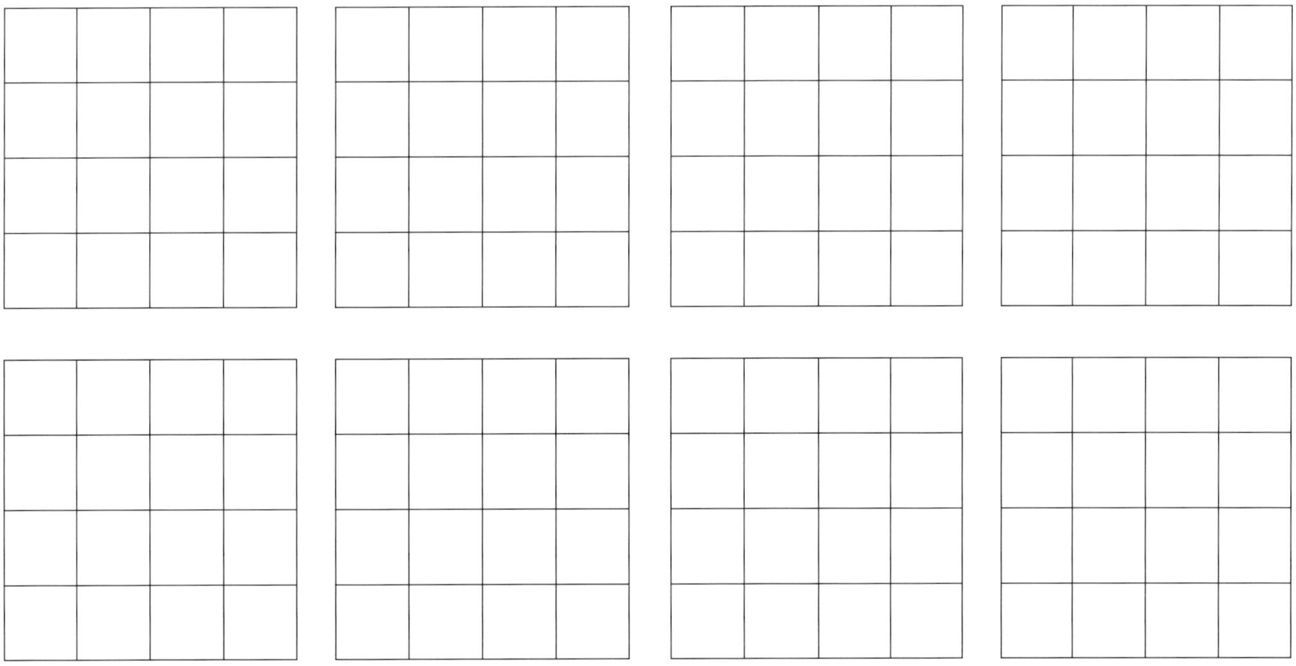

Name: ....

13c

Non-unitary fractions

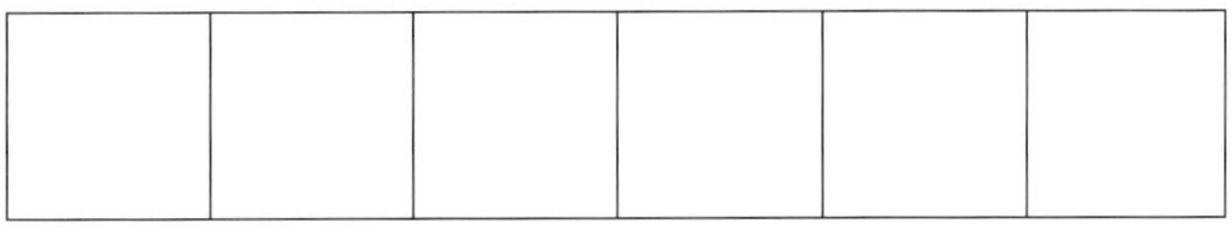

Colour $\frac{3}{5}$ of each shape.

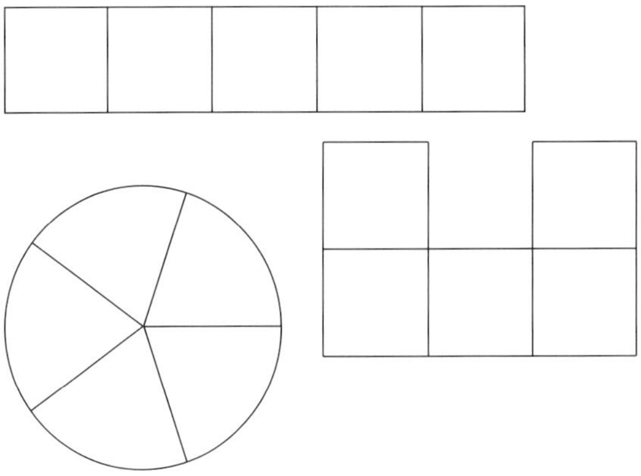

Colour $\frac{5}{8}$ of each shape.

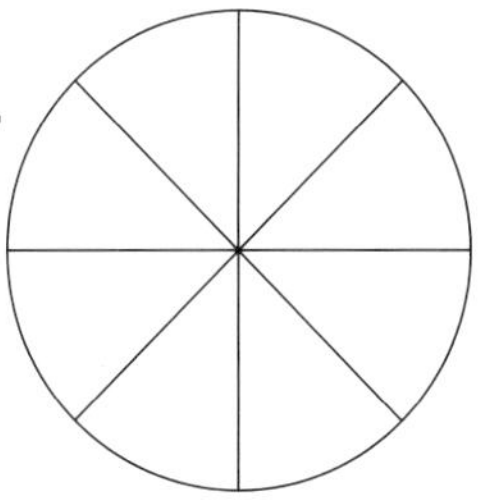

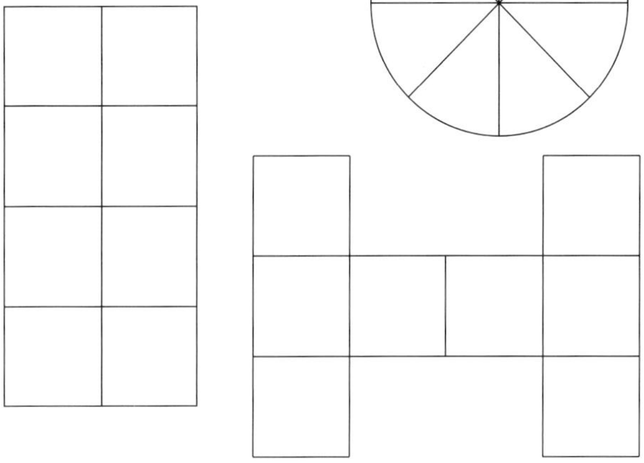

LESSON 14 Comparing and ordering fractions

Lesson objective

- to order simple fractions, for example, decide whether fractions such as $\frac{3}{8}$ or $\frac{7}{10}$ are greater or less than $\frac{1}{2}$

Language

- fraction, names for fractions, equivalent

Resources

- a number line on the board marked in 16 sections with the numbers 0 and 1 written at either end, **PCM14a, 14b, 14c**

Prior learning

- recognizing simple equivalent fractions
- comparing familiar fractions

Teaching

whole class: about 20 minutes

- Explain to the children that this lesson is about putting fractions in order of size.
- Ask them to count in halves to 5, starting at 0, for example, 'Zero, half, one, one and a half', and so on. Then count in quarters to 5 starting at 0, for example, 'Zero, quarter, half, three-quarters, one', and so on. Now count in eighths to 2, starting at 0.

  How many quarters make $\frac{1}{2}$? How many quarters make $1\frac{1}{2}$?

  Which is more, $\frac{3}{4}$ or $\frac{1}{2}$? Is $\frac{1}{8}$ bigger or smaller than $\frac{1}{4}$?

  How many eighths are equivalent to $\frac{3}{4}$?

  Which is greater, $\frac{3}{4}$ or $\frac{7}{8}$? Which is greater, $\frac{1}{2}$ or $\frac{5}{8}$?

- Look at the number line on the board and explain that it represents the range 0 to 1. Point to the mark half-way between 0 and 1.

  What number does this mark represent?

  Discuss the children's suggestions until they offer $\frac{1}{2}$, $\frac{4}{8}$ and $\frac{8}{16}$. Write these fractions below the mark. Repeat this for other points on the line, for example $\frac{1}{8}$, $\frac{1}{4}$, $\frac{3}{8}$, $\frac{1}{2}$, $\frac{5}{8}$, $\frac{3}{4}$ and $\frac{7}{8}$. Write the fraction immediately below the marks and also any equivalent fractions offered by the children directly below the simplest forms. So $\frac{2}{4}$ will be beneath $\frac{1}{2}$, and $\frac{4}{8}$ will be beneath $\frac{2}{4}$, and so on, for example:

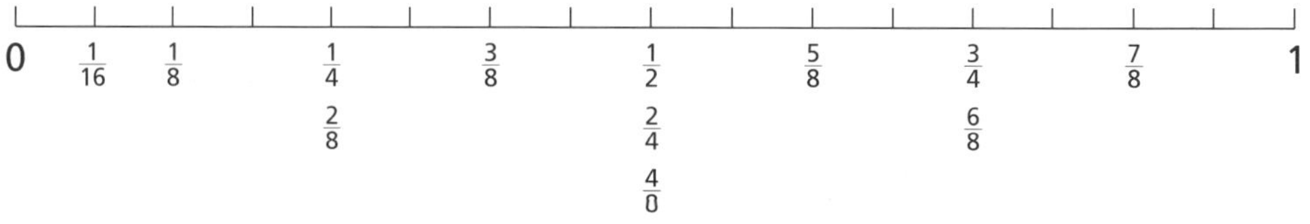

- Ask the children to supply any equivalent fractions which have not yet been recorded and add them to the number line. Look at the completed fraction line and compare the different fractions.

  Which fractions are equivalent to $\frac{1}{4}$? Is $\frac{1}{4}$ greater than or less than $\frac{1}{8}$ on this number line? Which fractions are greater than $\frac{1}{2}$?

Activities

about 15 minutes

Core (for whole class or average attainers)

Hand out **PCM14a**, and explain to the children that they will begin by shading shapes to show given fractions. They then write the equivalent fraction shown by the shape. Go through the first example with them to make sure they understand the activity. The second part of the **PCM** involves placing sets of fractions in order of size. Tell them they can use the fraction line on the board for help if they wish.

Extension (for extension lesson or higher attainers)

Tell the children that they will be writing all the fractions they can make using given numbers before listing them in order of size. Give them **PCM14b** and explain that they should make as many fractions as they can from the numbers given in the box (there are 28 in total). They can only make fractions where the top number is less than the bottom number so the fraction is less than 1. Explain that the blank number lines are there to help them order their work if they wish.

Support (for reinforcement lesson or lower attainers)

Give each child a copy of **PCM14c** and look at the first rectangle together. Ask them how many equal parts are shown and what fraction of the whole rectangle each part is ($\frac{1}{8}$). Ask them to draw a coloured line on the rectangle to divide it into halves.

Which is bigger, $\frac{1}{2}$ or $\frac{1}{8}$? How many eighths are the same as $\frac{1}{2}$?

Ask them to colour $\frac{1}{4}$ of the rectangle.

How many eighths are the same as $\frac{1}{4}$? How many quarters make $\frac{1}{2}$? Which is the smallest fraction? Which is the next smallest?

Look at the fractions written below the rectangle and ask the children to indicate each on the rectangle (by tracing round the fraction with a finger). Ask which is the smallest fraction, then the next smallest, and so on. Explain that they should write the three fractions in order of size in the space provided, before repeating the activity on the second rectangle.

Plenary

whole class: about 5 minutes

Look again at the number line on the board. Ask the children to suggest where fractions such as $\frac{1}{10}$, $\frac{1}{5}$, $\frac{7}{10}$ and $\frac{3}{10}$ should be placed, explaining that they won't lie exactly on a mark. Discuss the responses and mark them on the line. Then ask questions such as:

Which is greater, $\frac{1}{2}$ or $\frac{3}{5}$?

Further activities

- Give each child a fraction card showing different fractions, such as $\frac{1}{4}$, $\frac{1}{2}$, $\frac{2}{3}$, $\frac{2}{5}$, $\frac{3}{4}$, 1, $1\frac{3}{4}$, $1\frac{1}{3}$, and so on. Ask the children to place their cards on a number line or line the children up in the order of their fractions.
- To extend the activity, ask the children to find a partner/s to make a whole number such as 3 or 5.
- Make a set of cards showing the following fractions: $\frac{1}{2}$, $\frac{2}{4}$, $\frac{5}{10}$, $\frac{1}{4}$, $\frac{2}{8}$, $\frac{4}{8}$, $\frac{3}{6}$, $\frac{1}{5}$, $\frac{2}{10}$, $\frac{4}{4}$, $\frac{2}{2}$, $\frac{5}{5}$, $\frac{10}{10}$, 1
  Make some other cards with these fractions shown as a fraction of a shape.
  Use the cards for games and activities such as 'Snap' or 'Pelmanism', ordering a selection on a line so that equivalent fractions are in the same position; and a version of 'Happy Families' with fraction families being made.

Name: ....

14a

Comparing and ordering fractions

Colour and write the equivalent fractions.

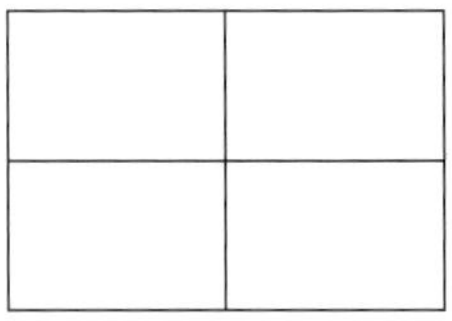

$\frac{1}{2} = \frac{\square}{\square}$

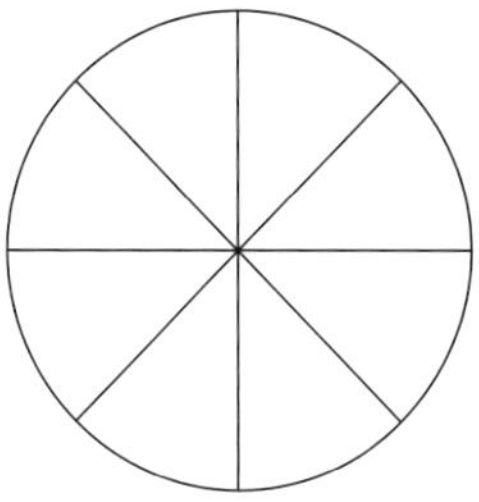

$\frac{1}{4} = \frac{\square}{\square}$

$\frac{1}{3} = \frac{\square}{\square}$

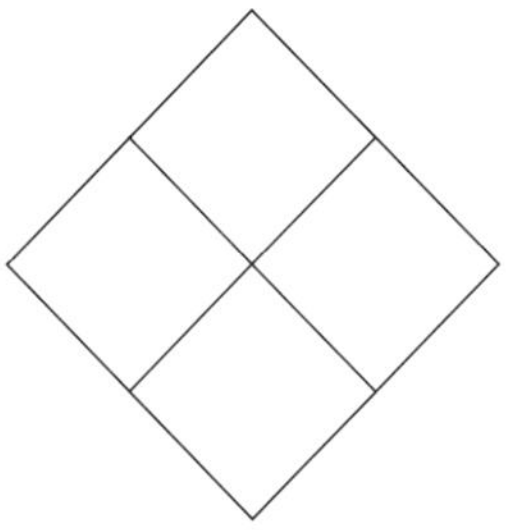

$\frac{1}{2} = \frac{\square}{\square}$

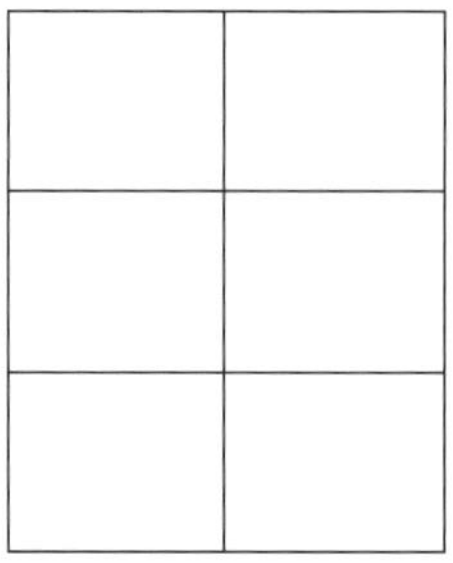

$\frac{1}{2} = \frac{\square}{\square}$

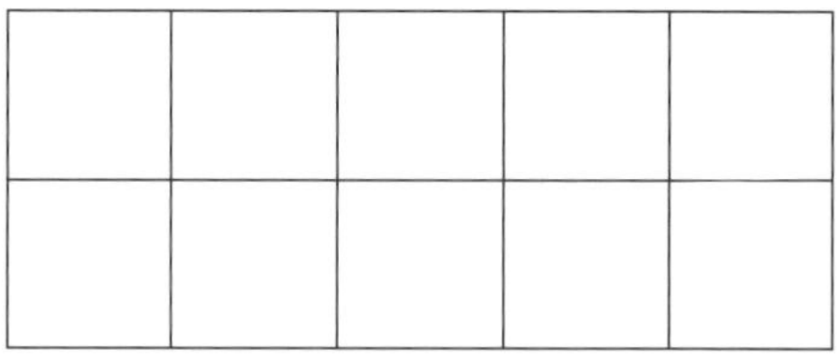

$\frac{1}{5} = \frac{\square}{\square}$

Write these sets of fractions in order of size, starting with the smallest.

$\frac{7}{8}$ $\frac{1}{2}$ $\frac{1}{4}$ $\frac{1}{8}$ $\frac{3}{8}$

$\frac{\square}{\square}$ $\frac{\square}{\square}$ $\frac{\square}{\square}$ $\frac{\square}{\square}$ $\frac{\square}{\square}$

$\frac{1}{10}$ $\frac{3}{5}$ $\frac{7}{10}$ $\frac{1}{5}$ $\frac{9}{10}$

$\frac{\square}{\square}$ $\frac{\square}{\square}$ $\frac{\square}{\square}$ $\frac{\square}{\square}$ $\frac{\square}{\square}$

$\frac{2}{3}$ $\frac{1}{3}$ $\frac{1}{2}$ $\frac{5}{6}$ $\frac{1}{6}$

$\frac{\square}{\square}$ $\frac{\square}{\square}$ $\frac{\square}{\square}$ $\frac{\square}{\square}$ $\frac{\square}{\square}$

$\frac{1}{12}$ $\frac{1}{2}$ $\frac{1}{6}$ $\frac{3}{4}$ $\frac{7}{12}$

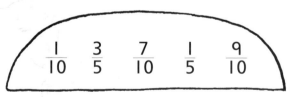

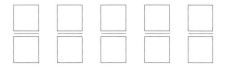

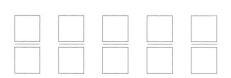

$\frac{\square}{\square}$ $\frac{\square}{\square}$ $\frac{\square}{\square}$ $\frac{\square}{\square}$ $\frac{\square}{\square}$

Name: ....

14b

Comparing and ordering fractions

- Use these numbers to make fractions.
- Each fraction must be less than 1.
- Write the fractions in order, starting with the smallest.

1 3 8 10 2 4 5 6

Name: ....

14c

Comparing and ordering fractions

Compare these fractions.

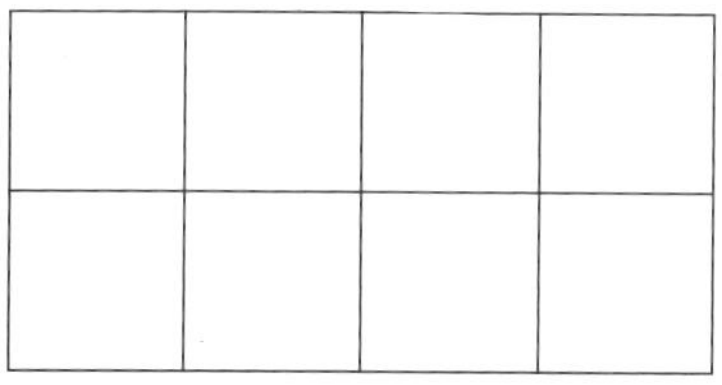

$\frac{1}{2}$ $\frac{1}{4}$ $\frac{1}{8}$

Smallest Largest

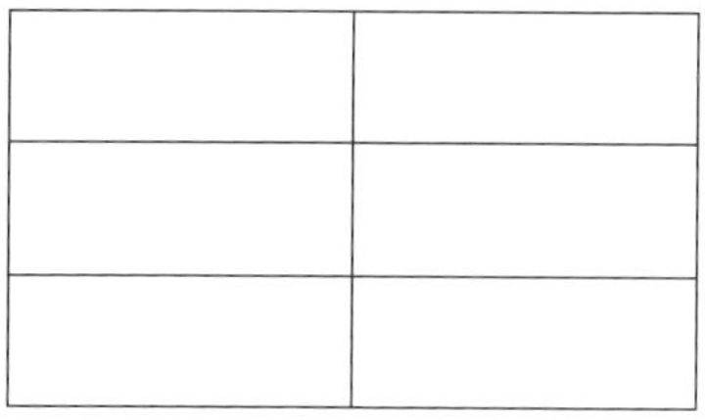

$\frac{1}{2}$ $\frac{1}{6}$ $\frac{1}{3}$

Smallest Largest

Key Lessons in Numeracy:
Numbers and the Number System Year 4

LESSON 15 Fractions totalling one

Lesson objective

- to identify two simple fractions which have a total of 1, for example, $\frac{3}{10}$ and $\frac{7}{10}$

Language

- total, fraction, names for fractions

Resources

- three large number lines drawn on the board (one marked in halves and quarters, the second marked in thirds and sixths, and the third marked in tenths and fifths, all lines the same length and each representing the range 0 to 1), **PCM15a, 15b, 15c**

Prior learning

- recognizing simple fractions which are several parts of a whole
- recognizing equivalent fractions

Teaching

whole class: about 20 minutes

- Explain to the children that this lesson is about finding two fractions which have a total value of 1.
- ***How many halves make 1?***

  Demonstrate this on the first number line by indicating each half and recording it on the board as $\frac{1}{2} + \frac{1}{2} = 1$.

  How many quarters make 1?

  Demonstrate this on the first number line, then ask a child to indicate $\frac{3}{4}$ of the line.

  How many more quarters are needed to make 1?

  Record this on the board as $\frac{3}{4} + \frac{1}{4} = 1$ and emphasize that 3 quarters and 1 quarter totals 4 quarters, which is 1 whole.
- Repeat the same activity, but this time using the second number line and using $\frac{2}{3} + \frac{1}{3} = 1$ and $\frac{5}{6} + \frac{1}{6} = 1$.

  Can you find a different pair of sixths which have a total of 1?

  Record the children's suggestions as equations on the board.

  How many sixths do we need altogether to make 1?

  Establish that in each of the equations, there is a total of 6 sixths.
- Now repeat the activity for fifths and tenths, with reference to the third number line.

Activities

about 20 minutes

Core (for whole class or average attainers)

Explain to the children that they will be showing fractions that total 1 using **PCM15a**. Show them how to complete the first example by estimating where the next line would be to divide the rectangle into the last two thirds. Write $\frac{1}{3}$ under each part and then complete the sum at the side.

Extension (for extension lesson or higher attainers)

Hand out **PCM15b** and tell the children that they will be investigating the different totals of one whole that can be made from thirds, quarters and twelfths. Read through the instructions and encourage them to display their findings in a clear and informative way.

Support (for reinforcement lesson or lower attainers)

Provide copies of **PCM15c**, pointing out to the children that they need to use two colours to show the fractions that total one whole. Go through the first example with them, asking them to colour $\frac{1}{3}$ red and $\frac{2}{3}$ blue. Show them that the whole circle is coloured, which shows that $\frac{2}{3} + \frac{1}{3} = 1$.

Plenary *whole class: about 10 minutes*

Say a fraction, such as $\frac{3}{5}$ and ask the children to supply the fraction which gives a total of 1 whole when added to it. Repeat this for other fractions. Remind the children that any two fractions with the same denominator have a total of 1 whole when their numerators total the number in the denominator.

Further activities

- Find pairs of fractions with a total of 1 whole using a 'fraction wall' diagram. Build a similar diagram using a computer art program and use it to find equivalent pairs, and pairs which total 1 whole, including fractions with different denominators.
- Ask the children to make a set of cards containing about 12 different pairs which have a total of 1 whole, one fraction per card. Use the set to play games such as 'Snap' and 'Pelmanism'. Alternatively, make a similar set of domino cards.

Name: **15a**

Fractions totalling one

Draw lines to show the missing fractions.
Write the fractions so that the total is 1.

$\frac{1}{3} + \square = 1$

$\frac{1}{4} + \square = 1$

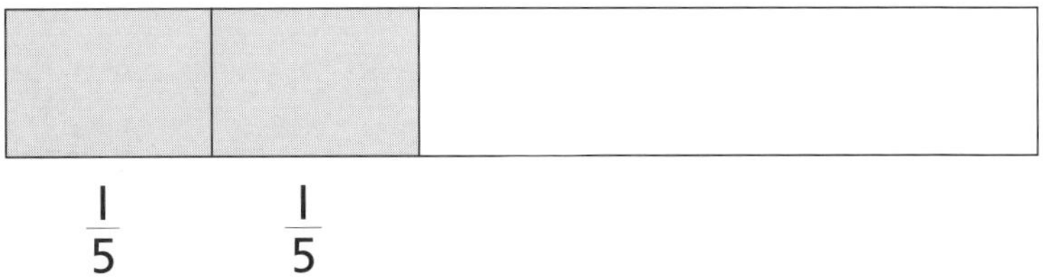

$\frac{2}{5} + \square = 1$

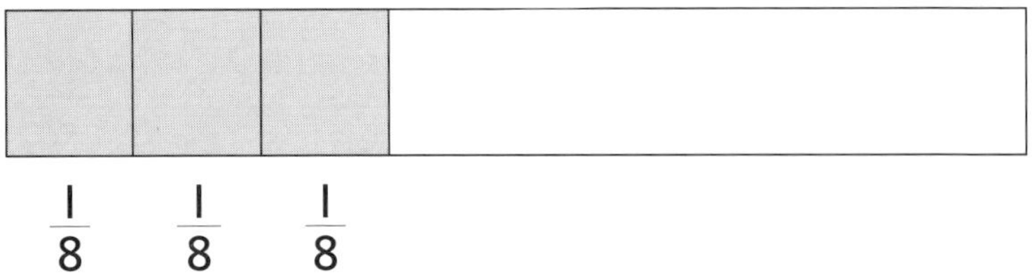

$\frac{3}{8} + \square = 1$

$\frac{3}{10} + \square = 1$

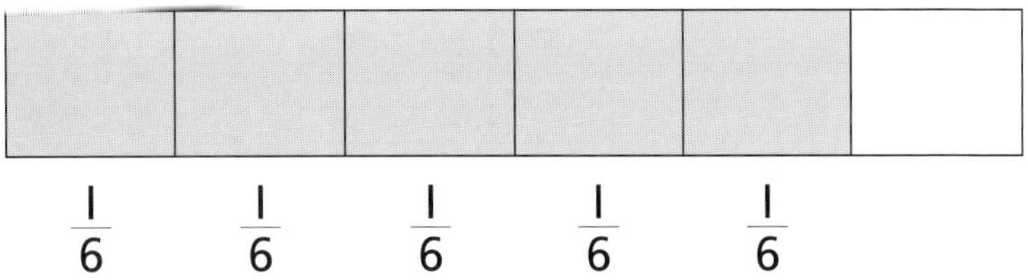

$\frac{5}{6} + \square = 1$

Draw a diagram to show that $\frac{7}{12} + \frac{5}{12} = 1$

Name: ....

15b

Fractions totalling one

This rod shows $\frac{1}{4} + \frac{1}{3} + \frac{5}{12} = 1$

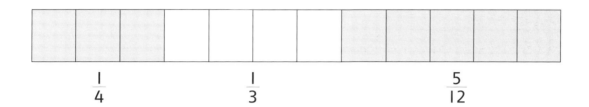

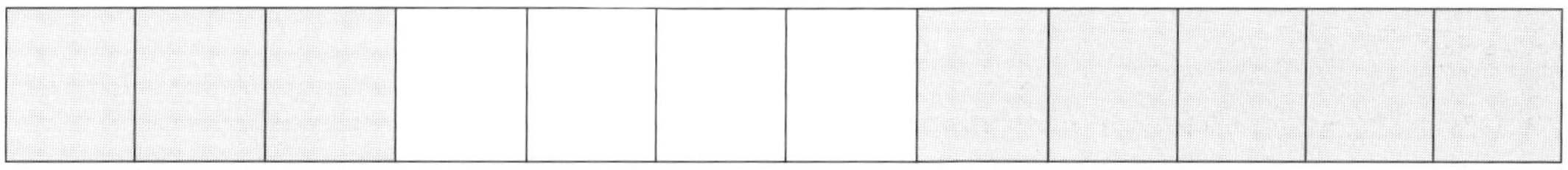

$\frac{1}{4}$ $\frac{1}{3}$ $\frac{5}{12}$

- Use strips of 12 squares to investigate other ways of totalling 1 whole using quarters, thirds and twelfths.
- Display your findings, clearly showing the different fractions and describing any patterns you see.

Name: ....

15c

Fractions totalling one

Use two colours to show these fractions that total 1.

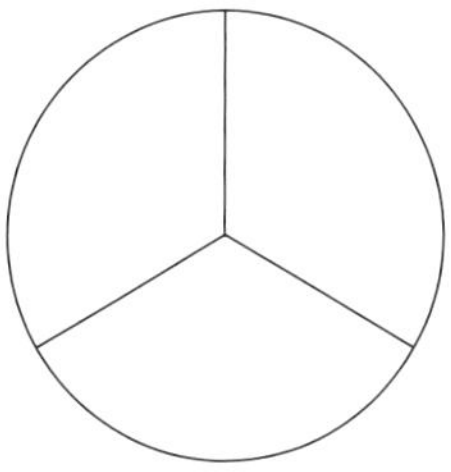

$\frac{1}{3} + \frac{2}{3} = 1$

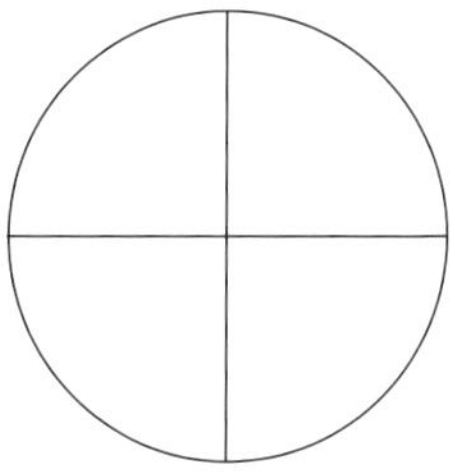

$\frac{1}{4} + \frac{3}{4} = 1$

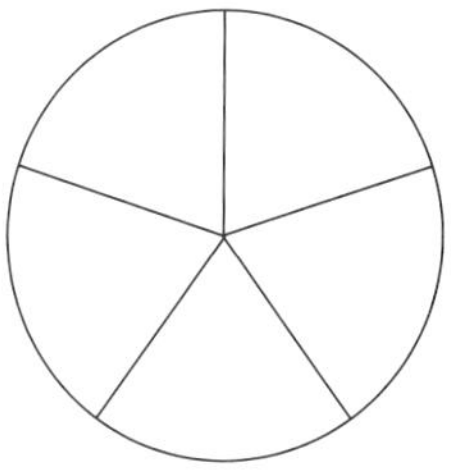

$\frac{2}{5} + \frac{3}{5} = 1$

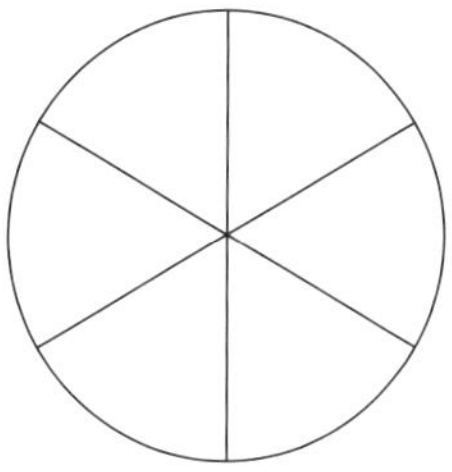

$\frac{1}{6} + \frac{\quad}{6} = 1$

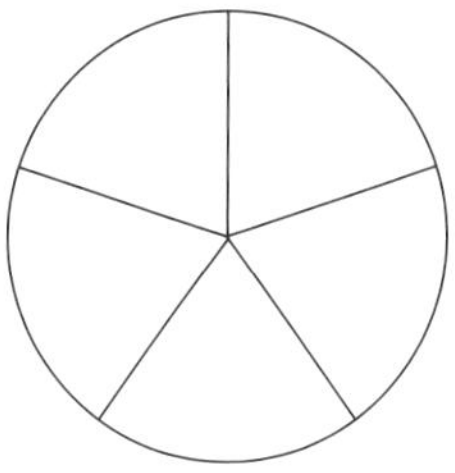

$\frac{4}{5} + \frac{\quad}{5} = 1$

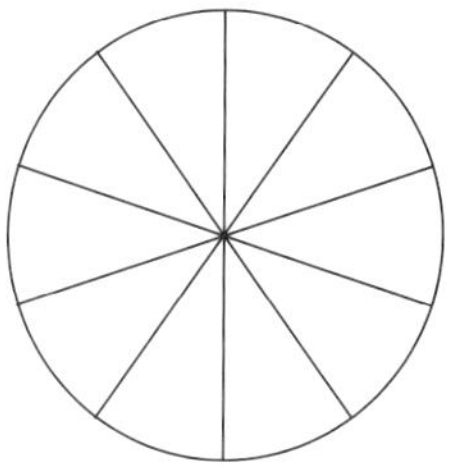

$\frac{3}{10} + \frac{\quad}{10} = 1$

LESSON 16 Fractions and division

Lesson objective

- to begin to relate fractions to division and find simple fractions of numbers or quantities

Language

- fraction, names for particular fractions

Resources

- cubes, individual fan numbers or digit cards (Resource sheets 1 and 2), collections of coins, interlocking cubes, **PCM16a, 16b, 16c**

Prior learning

- finding halves, quarters and thirds of numbers

Teaching ***whole class: about 20 minutes***

- Explain to the children that this lesson is about finding fractions of numbers and quantities.
- ***What is half of 8? What is half of 20? How did you work it out?***

  Establish that the answer is found by dividing by 2. Write $\frac{1}{2}$ on the board and remind the children that the number below the line shows how many equal parts the whole is divided into.
- Write $\frac{1}{4}$ on the board.

  How do we find a quarter of a number?

  Establish that the number would be divided by 4 because the 4 below the line tells us to do that. (If necessary, use interlocking cubes to model division, for instance 12 cubes into quarters and counting the number in each group.) Repeat this activity by finding different fractions of amounts.
- Ask the children to show you $\frac{1}{4}$ of multiples of 4 using their fan numbers or digit cards. Continue this for $\frac{1}{3}$, $\frac{1}{5}$ and $\frac{1}{10}$.

  Show me a quarter of 12, 20, 8, 16 and 40.

  Show me a third of 9, 15, 12, 21 and 27.

  Show me a fifth of 20, 30, 45, 15 and 40.

  Show me a tenth of 60, 90, 20, 50 and 70.

  Explain that the line in the fraction is used in the same way as a division sign – that $\frac{1}{2}$ means a 'whole' divided by 2. Make sure the children understand that in the questions above, they have been dividing the whole numbers by the bottom number of the fraction, or 4, 3, 5 and 10.
- Play 'Think of a number'.

  I am thinking of a number. Half of that number is 15. What number am I thinking of?

  Repeat the game for other fractions.

  I am thinking of a number. One quarter of that number is 3. What number am I thinking of?

  If children are finding this difficult, hold up 3 cubes and ask them to imagine that this is quarter of the whole amount, so they need 4 lots of the 3 cubes.

Activities ***about 15 minutes***

Core (for whole class or average attainers)

Give the children **PCM16a**. Point out that they need to find their way through the maze by answering the questions and following the correct route. They mark their route and collect a list of the answers so that they can eventually find the 'magic total' (which is 100).

Extension (for extension lesson or higher attainers)

Tell the children that they will be working out fractions of particular amounts of money. Hand out **PCM16b**. Suggest to the children that they can use coins to help them, if necessary, and remind them that it might be easier to convert the pounds to pence.

Support (for reinforcement lesson or lower attainers)

Give each child **PCM16c** and look at the first example together.

What is a half of 12? What is a quarter of 12? How did you work it out? Write your answers.

Discuss the responses and establish that $\frac{1}{4}$ can be found by dividing 12 by 4, or by asking 'How many fours make 12?'

What is a third of 12? Write the answer.

Discuss, as before, that reinforcing that a fraction of a number is found by dividing that number by the bottom number of the fraction.

Plenary ***whole class: about 5 minutes***

Ask the children to show you fractions of numbers using their fan numbers or digit cards. Remind them that they have been using division to find the answers and that fraction notation is another way of recording division.

Further activities

- Provide the children with some realistic problems which involve fractions of quantities such as:
  One third of the class have rolls instead of sandwiches. How many children is that?
  One fifth of the footballs are on the shed floor with the rest in the bags. If there are 20 footballs altogether, how many are in the bags?
- Investigate numbers which can be divided into different fractions, for example, 20 can be divided into halves, quarters, fifths, tenths and twentieths.
  Which numbers can you find which can be divided into five or more fractions?

Name: ....

Fractions and division

Find your way through the maze, collecting the correct answers as you go.

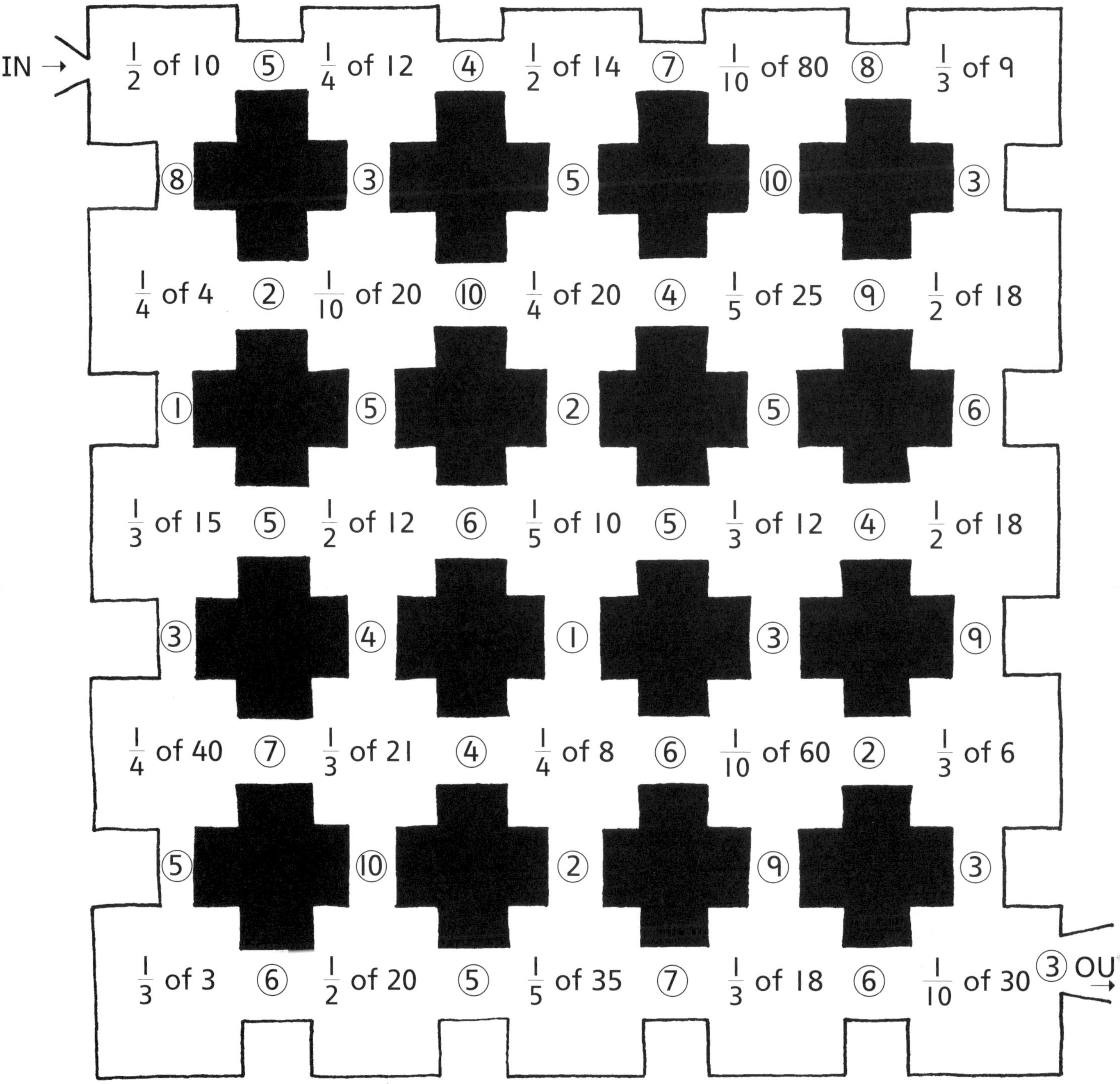

Now total your answers. The magic total is: ☐

Name: ....

16b

Fractions and division

Work out the fractions of these amounts.

£1·20

- $\frac{1}{2}$ →
- $\frac{1}{4}$ →
- $\frac{1}{3}$ →
- $\frac{1}{10}$ →
- $\frac{1}{5}$ →

£2·00

- $\frac{1}{2}$ →
- $\frac{1}{4}$ →
- $\frac{1}{10}$ →
- $\frac{1}{5}$ →

£1·80

- $\frac{1}{2}$ →
- $\frac{1}{3}$ →
- $\frac{1}{6}$ →
- $\frac{1}{10}$ →
- $\frac{1}{5}$ →

- -

Name: ....

16c

Fractions and division

$\frac{1}{2}$ of 12 =

$\frac{1}{4}$ of 12 =

$\frac{1}{3}$ of 12 =

Work out these fractions of amounts.
Use cubes to help you.

$\frac{1}{2}$ of 6 =

$\frac{1}{4}$ of 8 =

$\frac{1}{3}$ of 9 =

$\frac{1}{4}$ of 16 =

$\frac{1}{3}$ of 15 =

$\frac{1}{2}$ of 14 =

$\frac{1}{5}$ of 20 =

$\frac{1}{4}$ of 20 =

$\frac{1}{10}$ of 20 =

LESSON 17 Simple proportion

Lesson objective

- to begin to use ideas of simple proportion, for example, one for every and one in every

Language

- in every, for every

Resources

- a pattern of interlocking cubes in two different colours so that 1 in every 4 cubes is white, sets of interlocking cubes in two different colours for the children to use, squared paper, **PCM17a, 17b, 17c**

Prior learning

- understanding simple fractions

Teaching

whole class: about 20 minutes

- Explain to the children that this lesson is about solving simple problems involving numbers which have a particular relationship to each other.
- Begin by providing contexts for discussing ideas of simple proportion such as the following:

  Ask the children to look at their hands.

  How many fingers are there for every thumb? So how many fingers do you have for two thumbs? How many thumbs are there for eight fingers? How many fingers are there for six thumbs?

  Explain that the relationship between fingers and thumbs is 4 for every 1.

  In every week there are two weekend days. How many weekend days are there in three weeks? How many weeks contain eight weekend days?

  Explain that the relationship between weekend days and weeks is 2 in every 1.
- Write the numbers 1 to 10 on the board. Ask a child to put a ring around each odd number. Explain that when all the numbers are written one after the other in this way they are called consecutive numbers, and that 1 in every 2 consecutive numbers is odd.

  How many odd numbers are there in ten consecutive numbers? How many odd numbers are there in 20 consecutive numbers?
- Show the children the pattern of cubes.

  How many white cubes are there in every four cubes? How many red cubes are there in every four cubes? How many red cubes are there for every white cube?
- Ask the children to make a pattern with their cubes so that 1 in every 3 cubes is a particular colour. Continue this, asking them to make a pattern which illustrates 2 for every 3.

Activities ***about 20 minutes***

Core (for whole class or average attainers)

Give the children **PCM17a**, explaining that they need to colour the rows of tiles in the proportions shown, using an interesting pattern if possible. They then complete the proportions table.

Extension (for extension lesson or higher attainers)

Tell the children they will be using **PCM17b** to carry out an investigation into the arrangement of shaded squares with a proportion of 2 in 3 squares shaded. Complete the first two arrangements with this group and then ask them to use squared paper to investigate the arrangements with a row of 6 squares.

Support (for reinforcement lesson or lower attainers)

Hand out **PCM17c**, explaining to the children that they need to use cubes to make rectangle patterns with given proportions. They then colour the rectangles to show the patterns.

Plenary ***whole class: about 10 minutes***

Ask the group who completed **PCM17b** to show their work and explain the patterns they found in the investigation. Those that worked on **PCM17c** can show their cube patterns, asking the other children to give the proportions each shows.

Further activities

- Provide some problem-solving activities which involve 'in every' or 'for every'. For example:
  For every five 20p pieces, there are two 50p pieces. How many 20p pieces do I need for four 50p pieces? Five 50p pieces? Six 50p pieces?
  In a box of biscuits, two in every six biscuits is chocolate. How many chocolate biscuits are there if there are 30 biscuits altogether?

Name: ....

Simple proportion

Colour these squares to show the following proportions.

1 in every 2 squares red.

1 in every 5 squares blue.

1 in every 4 squares red.

3 in every 4 squares blue.

1 in every 3 squares red.

2 in every three squares blue.

Some red and blue cubes were joined together.

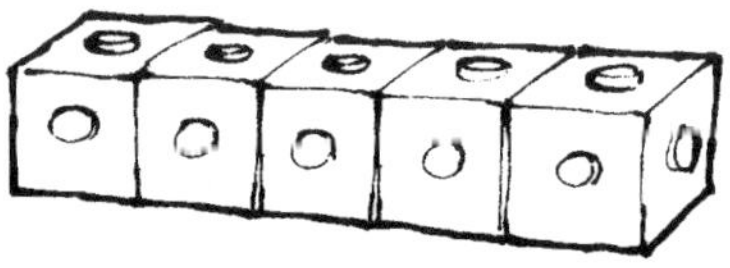

The proportions of red cubes is:

3 in every 5 cubes red

Complete the table.

Total number of cubes	Red cubes	Blue cubes
5		
10		
	9	
		8
25		
	18	

Name: 17b

Simple proportion

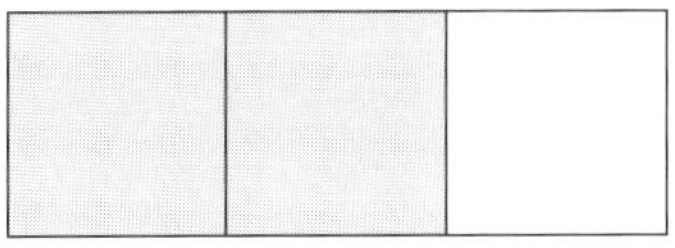

2 in 3 of these squares are shaded.

Shade these squares in two different patterns to show 2 in 3.

- Investigate the patterns that can be made using 6 squares, with a proportion of 2 in 3 squares shaded.

Investigate other numbers and proportions in your book.

Name: 17c

Simple proportion

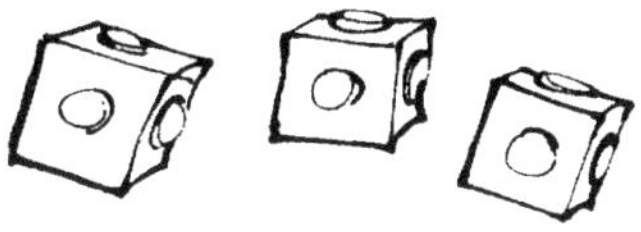

Use cubes to make rectangle patterns with these proportions.
Colour the rectangles to show your patterns.

1 in every 2 cubes red

1 in every 4 cubes green

2 in every 3 cubes yellow

2 in every 5 cubes blue

LESSON 18 Decimals and tenths

Lesson objective

- to understand the decimal notation for tenths
- to recognize the equivalence between the decimal and fraction forms of the tenths

Language

- decimal, decimal point, decimal place, decimal fraction

Resources

- counting stick, metre stick, ruler, tape measure, **PCM18a, 18b, 18c**

Prior learning:

- recognizing and using decimal notation for pounds and metres
- understanding place value in whole numbers
- Year 4 work on fractions

Teaching

whole class: about 20 minutes

- Explain to the children that this lesson is about reading and using decimal fractions
- Hold up the counting stick and tell the children that one end is 0 and the other end is 1. Ask what each of the marks represents. Emphasize that the stick is divided into tenths, so each mark is $\frac{1}{10}$ or 0·1. Point to each mark in turn on the stick. As you do, ask the children to count aloud in tenths, saying $\frac{1}{10}$, $\frac{2}{10}$, $\frac{3}{10}$, and so on. Point to random positions on the stick, asking what fraction it represents. Repeat this activity, but this time name each position as decimal tenths, so 0·1, 0·2, 0·3, and so on. Ensure they recognize the relationship between the fraction and decimal, for example, that $\frac{7}{10}$ is the same as 0.7.
- Write $\frac{3}{10}$ on the board.

  How can we write this as a decimal fraction?

  Establish that there are no whole units and that the decimal fraction is 'zero point three' and this is recorded as 0·3. Explain that we put 0 in the units place to draw attention to the decimal point, otherwise it might be overlooked. Write $\frac{7}{10}$ on the board and ask one child to record and read it as a decimal fraction. Repeat this for one or two more tenths.
- Remind the children that they already know how to use decimal notation for money and length. Write 2·5m on the board.

  What does that say? What does it mean?

  Make sure the children are clear it represents 2m and 50cm.
- Write $2\frac{1}{2}$m on the board.

  What does that say? What does it mean? How many centimetres make 1 metre? What fraction of 1m is 50cm?

  Establish that 2·5m is the same as $2\frac{1}{2}$m because 50cm is half a metre.
- ***How many 10cm make 1m? What fraction of 1m is 10cm?***

  Establish that there are 100cm in 1m, so 10cm is $\frac{1}{10}$m.
- Write 2·1m on the board.

  What does that say? What does it mean?

  Establish that 2·1m means 2m and 10cm, which is $2\frac{1}{10}$m.

Activities ***about 15 minutes***

Core (for whole class or average attainers)

Tell the children that they will be practising recording tenths fractions in words, mixed fractions and decimal fractions. Give out **PCM18a** and talk through the activities to make sure the children are clear about what is required.

Extension (for extension lesson or higher attainers)

Hand out **PCM18b** and explain to the children that they will be using a metre stick, a ruler and a tape measure to measure the length of different objects around the classroom. Make sure they understand how to round to the nearest 10cm before beginning the activity.

Support (for reinforcement lesson or lower attainers)

Give each child a copy of **PCM18c** and point out that the aim is to match decimals and fractions. Start the children off by looking at 1·8 and asking them to find its equivalent fraction. Remind them that the digit after the decimal point shows tenths, so this is 1 and $\frac{8}{10}$. Write this on the board before asking them to colour both equivalents in the same colour. They continue this for the other pairs, writing the two missing fractions (one decimal and one fraction) before colouring the final two pairs.

Plenary ***whole class: about 5 minutes***

Write some pairs of numbers on the board, for example:

3·2 1·6 *0·9 3·5* *1·2 0·5* *2·8 0·3*

Take each pair in turn and ask the children to read the numbers aloud together. Which is the smaller number? How do they know?

Look at the first two pairs together so you work with four numbers.

Which is the smallest number? Which comes next in order of size? Which next? Which is the biggest number?

Repeat this for the other two pairs. Finally, order all eight numbers from the smallest to the largest.

Further activities

- Play 'Decimal lines'. The children use a ruler marked in millimetres to draw accurately a line of 10cm. They then mark positions at specified lengths along the line from the start, for example:
  3·3cm 1·8cm 2·6cm 0·7cm ?
  The children then measure the remaining length to check their accuracy (1·6cm)
- Give each child a card strip marked in ten equal sections on one side and blank on the other. Wrap an elastic band round it to slide along the strip. Ask some questions that involve tenths, for example:
  If one end is 0 and the other end is 1, show me the position of 0·6, 0·5, 0·2, 0·9, and so on.
  Continue this activity using different end numbers, perhaps 3 and 4, 6 and 7.

Name: ....

Decimals and tenths

Complete this table.

0·6	→	$\frac{6}{10}$	→	six tenths
	→		→	three tenths
	→	$\frac{9}{10}$	→	
0·1	→		→	
	→		→	two and seven tenths
1·5	→		→	
	→	$1\frac{3}{10}$	→	
2·8	→		→	

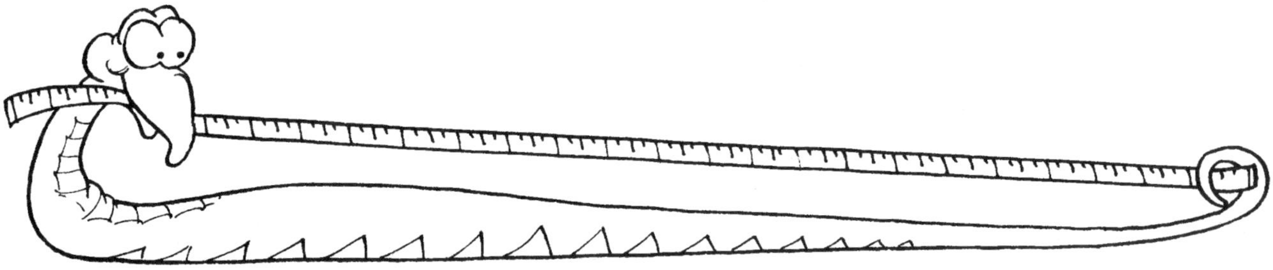

Write the fractions and decimals shown on this number line.

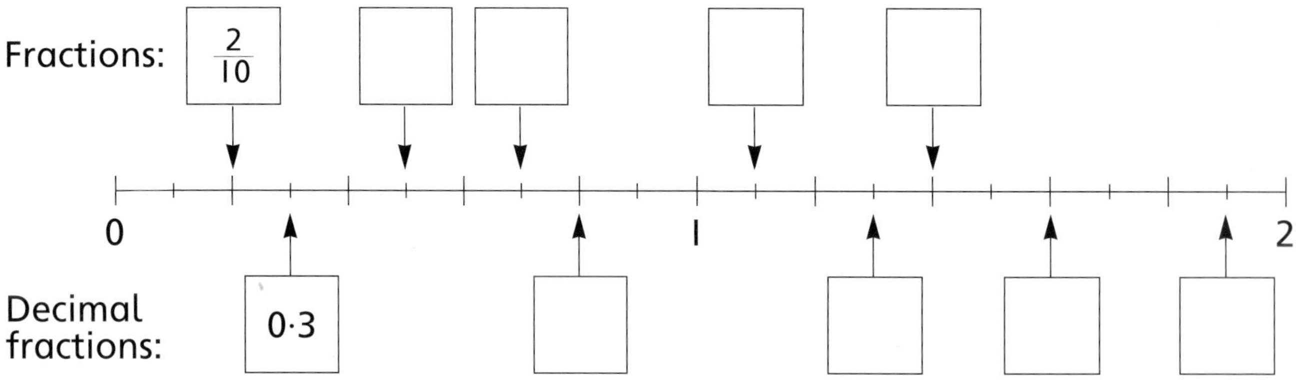

Name: ....

18b

Decimals and tenths

Measure and record the length of different objects in the classroom.
Round each length to the nearest 10cm.

Object	Length (_m _cm)	Decimal length	Length as a fraction
table	1m 10cm	1·1m	$1\frac{1}{10}$m

Name: ....

18c

Decimals and tenths

Match the equivalent fractions and decimals.
Colour in the pairs.
Write the missing fractions.

$\frac{7}{10}$

1·6

$1\frac{8}{10}$

0·8

1·8

$\frac{9}{10}$

0·7

$\frac{8}{10}$

$1\frac{6}{10}$

1·4

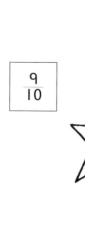

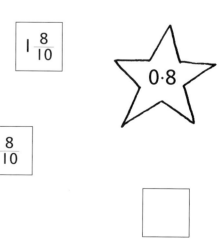

LESSON 19 Decimals and money

Lesson objective

- to use decimal notation in the context of money
- to order amounts of money and convert a sum of money, such as £13·25, to pence

Language

- decimal notation, decimal point, decimal place

Resources

- money arrow cards (Resource sheet 6), **PCM19a, 19b, 19c**

Prior learning

- recognizing and using decimal notation for pounds and metres
- understanding place value in whole numbers to one decimal place
- using decimal fractions to one decimal place

Teaching ***whole class: about 20 minutes***

- Explain to the children that they are going to learn more about using decimal recording in the context of money in this lesson.
- Write 235p on the board.

  What does that say? What does it mean? How many pounds are there? How do we normally record amounts of money when there are pounds?

  Discuss the responses and write £2·35 on the board. Explain that when we use decimal notation for recording money, we read it incorrectly. It should say 'two point three five pounds' because that is the correct way to read decimals, but in everyday use people say 'two pounds thirty-five'. This is because the decimal point separates the pounds from the pence. Remind the children that the first decimal place has a value of tenths.

  How many pence make £1? How many 10p pieces make £1?
- Point again to the £2·35 on the board.

  What does the 2 mean in this? What does the 3 mean?

  What does the 5 mean?

  Make sure the children recognize that the 2 is £2, the 3 is 30p and the 5 is 5p. With money, there are always 2 digits after the decimal, point, so £2·4 should be written as £2·40, with a 0 in the empty column. Remind the children not to write £2·40**p**.
- Say different amounts of money as pounds and pence for the children to show using their money arrow cards.

  Show me £1·45. Show me 50p more than this.

  Show me £2·09. What is 10p less than this?

  Develop this activity by giving amounts of money as pence, asking the children to use their money arrow cards to show them as pounds and pence, for example:

  Show me three hundred and twenty-two pence.

  Repeat for other amounts.
- Write £1·60 and £1·06 on the board.

  Which is the smallest amount of money? How do you know?

  Repeat this for other pairs such as £2·75 and £5·72, £3·80 and £3·08, and £0·99 and £9·90.

Activities *about 15 minutes*

Core (for whole class or average attainers)

Hand out **PCM19a**, explaining it includes questions about a copy of a receipt from a supermarket. Once they have answered these in their book, they should write the list of items in the box in order of price on a blank receipt, starting with the item with the lowest price.

Extension (for extension lesson or higher attainers)

Tell the children that they will be investigating the different amounts that can be made from three digits and a decimal point, where the decimal point appears after the first digit only. Hand out **PCM19b** and read through the investigation with them. Make sure they record the results in their book. This activity can be developed by providing four digits and asking the children to record all the different amounts, again with the decimal always after the first digit.

Support (for reinforcement lesson or lower attainers)

Give each child a copy of **PCM19c** and explain that they should rewrite the amounts of money given as pence in decimal notation, then put the amounts in order. They can use their money arrow cards to help them.

Plenary *whole class: about 5 minutes*

Ask the children who completed **PCM19b** to explain their results to the class. Which were the highest and lowest amounts from the three digits? Go through the second part of **PCM**, asking the children to read out the prices in order.

Remind the children that they have been learning more about decimal recording for money and explain that money is almost always recorded in this way in everyday life. Ask them to take notice of how prices are shown next time they go shopping.

Further activities

- Ask the children to use some holiday brochures to plan a family holiday for under £500. Vary the number of members in the family each time.
- Encourage the children to use a calculator to check totals of till receipts, making sure they use the decimal key. Remind them that the calculator will show £3·60 as 3·6 and £10·80 as 10·8. Encourage them to read the running totals as pounds and pence.

Name: ....

Decimals and money

bread	£0·65
butter	£1·03
orange juice	£2·59
cheese	£4·66
toilet roll	£3·97
sausages	£2·72
ham	£3·18
milk	£0·89
Total	£19·69
Received	£20·00
Change	

Use the receipt to answer these questions in your book.

1. Which is the most expensive item?
2. Which items are between 50p and £1?
3. Which item costs 103p?
4. Which item is nearest in price to £4?
5. How much does the bread and butter cost together?
6. How much change will be given from £20?

Total	£16·63

Use this blank receipt to write the following prices in order, starting with the lowest price.

- sticky tape £0·76
- 5 pencils £1·08
- glue £1·27
- envelopes £4·63
- writing paper £2·45
- paperclips £0·92
- ink pen £2·19
- 4 folders £3·33

Name: ....

19b

Decimals and money

- The digits 1 6 5 can make £1·65.

  They can also make £6·15, £1·56, £5·61, and so on.

- If the rule is that the decimal point always comes after the first digit, which other numbers can be made?

- Using the same rule, investigate all the amounts that can be made from 4 2 7

  Remember, the rule is that the decimal point comes after the first digit.

  Write the amounts in order in your book.

Name: ....

19c

Decimals and money

example:

485p → £4·85

Write these as decimal money.

140p →	225p →	308p →
250p →	380p →	219p →
85p →	104p →	195p →
200p →	231p →	205p →

Now write these amounts in order, starting with the lowest price.

LESSON 20 Rounding decimals

Lesson objective

- to round a sum of money to the nearest pound

Language

- digit, nearest, approximately, approximation, decimal notation, decimal point

Resources

- money arrow cards (Resource sheet 6), shopping catalogue, **PCM20a, 20b, 20c**

Prior learning

- recognizing and using decimal notation for measurements and costs
- rounding numbers to the nearest 10 or 100

Teaching

whole class: about 20 minutes

- Explain to the children that this lesson is about rounding money to the nearest pound. Remind them that they already know how to round numbers to the nearest 10 or 100.

  What is 372 to the nearest 10? How did you work it out? What is it to the nearest 100? Which digit did you think about when you worked that out? What is the rule for rounding numbers up or down?

  Establish that numbers are rounded up when the digit is 5 or greater than 5, and rounded down when the digit is less than 5.

- Write £9·99 on the board and explain that prices like this are often seen in shops.

  If you bought a T-shirt which cost £9·99, how much change would you get from £10·00? So what is £9·99 to the nearest pound? Why do you think shops use prices like this?

  Discuss the responses and establish that these prices make the items seem less expensive than they really are. We pay more attention to the pounds than we do to the pence, and so £9-something seems a lot less than £10.

- Write £3·75 on the board.

  What is that to the nearest pound? Which digit did you consider when you worked it out? Why?

  Establish that rounding to the nearest £1 is similar to rounding a number to the nearest 100 – we consider the digit immediately to the right of the digit we are rounding to and use the rounding rule. So 268 rounds to 300 and £2·68 rounds to £3. Decimal notation works in the same way as the decimal point does not make any difference to the rule.

- Ask the children to use their money arrow cards to show different amounts you say, and then approximate them to the nearest £1. Include some figures to be rounded up and some down.

  Show me £2·15. Round this to the nearest £1 and show me the amount.

  Show me £4·61. Now round this to the nearest £1.

  Show me £1·89, £4·09, £2·48, £3·50. Now round them to the nearest £1.

- Point out to the children that many people use approximation like this when they are shopping. Each item is rounded to the nearest £1 as it is selected and the total number of pounds held mentally to get a rough idea of how much the total will be.

  Why do you think they approximate using rounding to do this? Why not do it accurately?

  Establish that approximation is easier to handle mentally and that, in this situation, an approximation is sufficient for most people.

Activities

about 15 minutes

Give the children **PCM20a**. Make sure they understand the activity, emphasizing particularly the requirements for approximation by rounding up or down to the nearest £1.

Extension (for extension lesson or higher attainers)

Ask the children to list ten items and their prices from some pages of a shopping catalogue. They then write the rounded price alongside. The rule is that they must not go over a total of £100. Hand out **PCM20b**, making sure they understand the activity before they begin.

Support (for reinforcement lesson or lower attainers)

Work orally with this group to round costs up or down to the nearest £1, emphasizing the rule and using the money arrow cards as reinforcement. Give each child a copy of **PCM20c** and explain that they should write each cost to the nearest £1.

Plenary

whole class: about 5 minutes

Discuss the approximate total for the shopping bill on **PCM20a**. What total did the children find? (It should be approximately £24.) Ask the children who completed **PCM20b** to list the items they bought, and how much they came to in total. Reinforce the fact that when we go shopping, it is useful to have an approximate total cost for the items we are buying, and rounding to the nearest £1 is the easiest way to do this.

Further activities

- Play 'Money rounding' in pairs. Player A inputs a calculation, such as *£5·63 + £3·87* or *£4·91 – £1·07*, into their calculator. They ask Player B to give an answer to the calculation, rounded to the nearest £1. This is then checked with the calculator, with a point given for a correct answer. Each player takes turns, with the first to, say, 10 points being the winner.
- To extend the activity, the answers can be rounded to the nearest 10p.

Name: ....

20a

Rounding decimals

yoghurt	£1·09
soup	£0·75
washing powder	£4·81
soap	£1·55
toothpaste	£2·87
apples	£1·47
cheese	£3·80
lemonade	£1·70
pizza	£4·19
tomatoes	£1·40
Total	

Use the receipt to answer these questions.

1. Which item costs approximately £5? ☐

2. What is the approximate price of the toothpaste? ☐

3. What is the approximate total of the pizza and the lemonade? ☐

4. What is the approximate price of the yoghurt? ☐

I think the bill is about £28.

5. Is Mr Harris correct? Work out the approximate total for the shopping bill. ☐

Now choose some of the items on the receipt to make an approximate total of £10.

Name: 20b

Rounding decimals

You will need: a shopping catalogue

- Choose ten items from the catalogue and list them.
- Round each price to the nearest pound.
- What is your total? Your total approximate price must not go over £100.

How close to £100 can you get?

Name: 20c

Rounding decimals

Round these amounts to the nearest £ (pound).

example:

£1·20 → £1

£1·80 →	£4·25 →	£2·60 →
£3·55 →	£5·09 →	£3·50 →
£4·49 →	£2·62 →	£2·01 →
£5·69 →	£1·51 →	£3·39 →

Resource sheet 1 Fan numbers

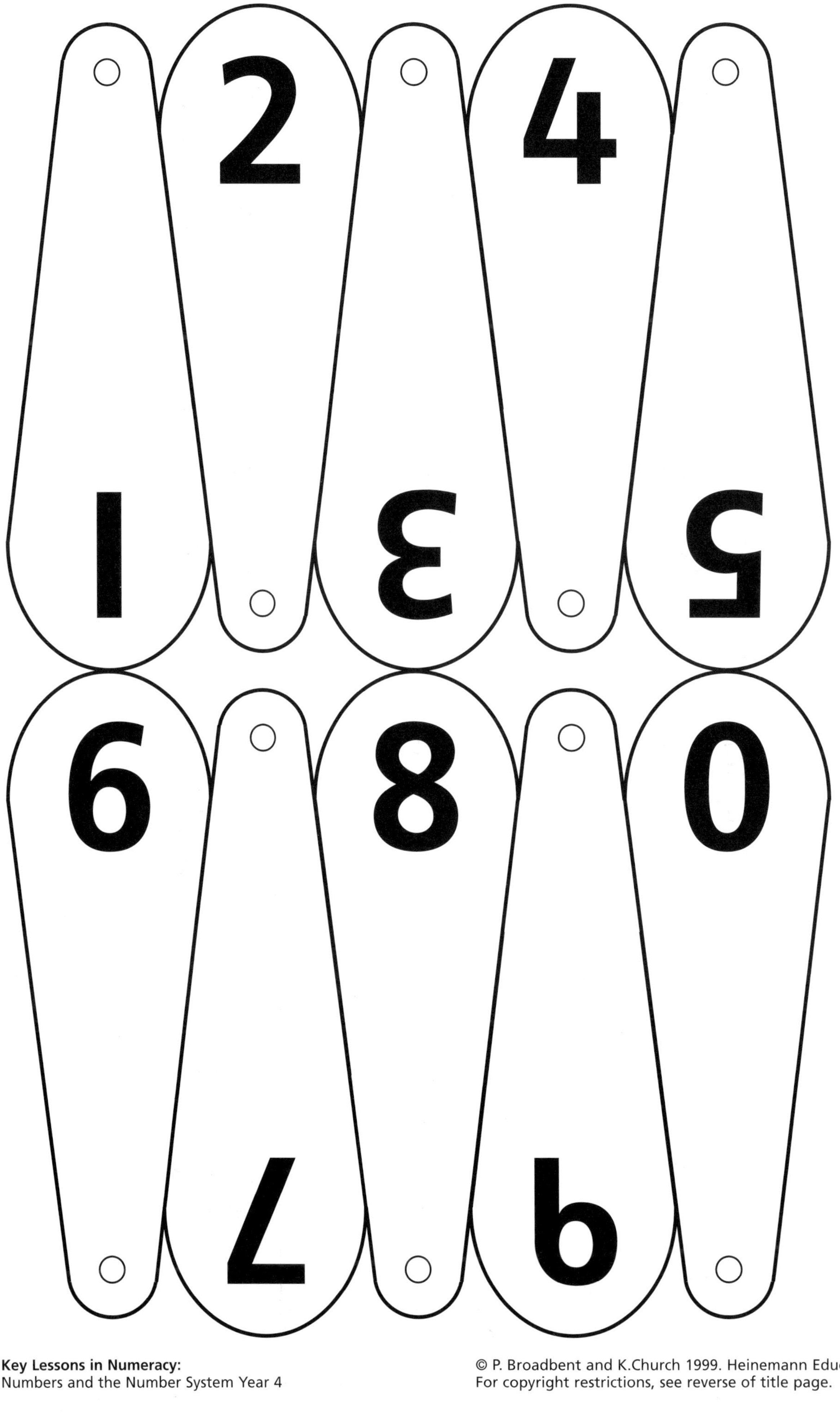

Resource sheet 2 Digit cards

0	1	2
3	4	5
6	7	8
–	9	0

Resource sheet 3 1–100 squares

1	2	3	4	5	6	7	8	9	10
11	12	13	14	15	16	17	18	19	20
21	22	23	24	25	26	27	28	29	30
31	32	33	34	35	36	37	38	39	40
41	42	43	44	45	46	47	48	49	50
51	52	53	54	55	56	57	58	59	60
61	62	63	64	65	66	67	68	69	70
71	72	73	74	75	76	77	78	79	80
81	82	83	84	85	86	87	88	89	90
91	92	93	94	95	96	97	98	99	100

1	2	3	4	5	6	7	8	9	10
11	12	13	14	15	16	17	18	19	20
21	22	23	24	25	26	27	28	29	30
31	32	33	34	35	36	37	38	39	40
41	42	43	44	45	46	47	48	49	50
51	52	53	54	55	56	57	58	59	60
61	62	63	64	65	66	67	68	69	70
71	72	73	74	75	76	77	78	79	80
81	82	83	84	85	86	87	88	89	90
91	92	93	94	95	96	97	98	99	100

Resource sheet 4 Number grids

①

0	1	2	3	4
5	6	7	8	9
10	11	12	13	14
15	16	17	18	19
20	21	22	23	24

②

0	1	2	3	4	5
6	7	8	9	10	11
12	13	14	15	16	17
18	19	20	21	22	23
24	25	26	27	28	29
30	31	32	33	34	35

③

1	2	3	4
5	6	7	8
9	10	11	12
13	14	15	16

④

0	1	2	3	4	5	6
7	8	9	10	11	12	13
14	15	16	17	18	19	20
21	22	23	24	25	26	27
28	29	30	31	32	33	34
35	36	37	38	39	40	41
42	43	44	45	46	47	48

⑤

1	2	3	4	5	6
7	8	9	10	11	12
13	14	15	16	17	18
19	20	21	22	23	24
25	26	27	28	29	30
31	32	33	34	35	36

⑥

1	2	3	4	5
6	7	8	9	10
11	12	13	14	15
16	17	18	19	20
21	22	23	24	25

Resource sheet 5 Arrow cards

1000	900	10	9
2000	800	20	8
3000	700	30	7
4000	600	40	6
5000	500	50	5
6000	400	60	4
7000	300	70	3
8000	200	80	2
9000	100	90	1

Resource sheet 6 Decimal money arrow cards

£1·00	90	1
£2·00	80	2
£3·00	70	3
£4·00	60	4
£5·00	50	5
£6·00	40	6
£7·00	30	7
£8·00	20	8
£9·00	10	9

Name: **1a**

Reading and writing numbers to 10 000

Write these both as numbers and as words.

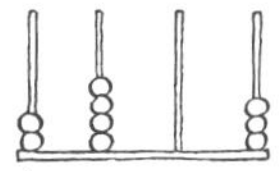
Th H T U

two thousand, four hundred and three

2403

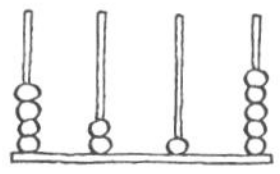
Th H T U

four thousand, two hundred and fifteen

4215

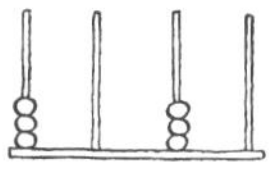
Th H T U

three thousand and thirty

3030

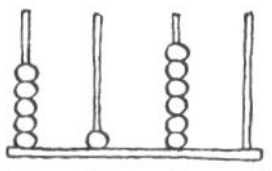
Th H T U

five thousand, one hundred and sixty

5160

Th H T U

one thousand and six

1006

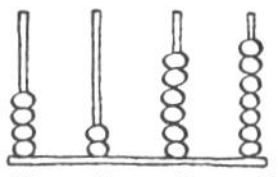
Th H T U

four thousand, two hundred and sixty-seven

4267

Name: **1b**

Reading and writing numbers to 10 000

You need: some counters, 0–9 digit cards

- Shuffle the digit cards.
- Pick any four cards.
- Make a 4-digit number from the cards. Place counters on the abacus to show the number.
- Write the number in your book as a word and a numeral.
- Make as many different numbers as you can from the four digits.

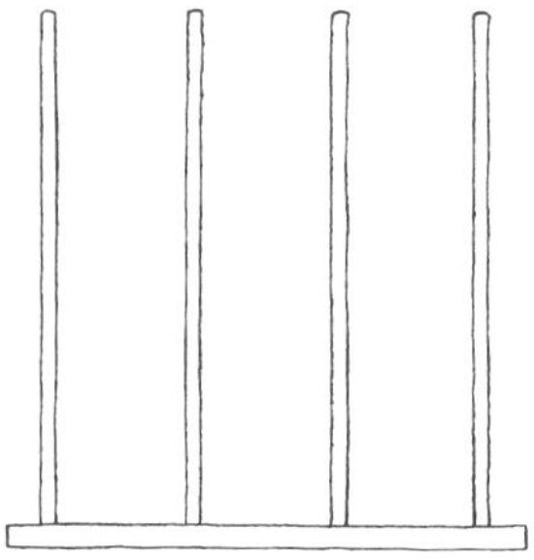

Name: **1c**

Reading and writing numbers to 10 000

Write the missing numbers in words or figures.

- 2487 two thousand, four hundred and eighty-seven
- 4018 four thousand and eighteen
- 3040 three thousand and forty
- 4250 four thousand, two hundred and fifty
- 4206 four thousand, two hundred and six
- 2000 two thousand
- 4675 four thousand, six hundred and seventy-five
- 8063 eight thousand and sixty-three

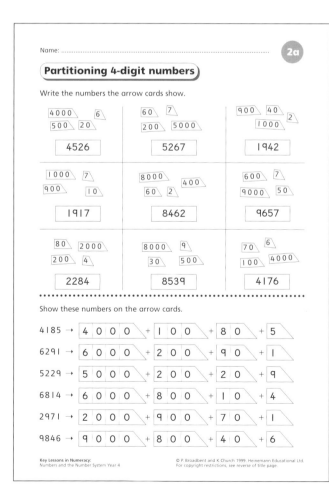

Name: **2a**

Partitioning 4-digit numbers

Write the numbers the arrow cards show.

4000, 6, 500, 20 → 4526	60, 7, 200, 5000 → 5267	900, 40, 2, 1000 → 1942
1000, 7, 900, 10 → 1917	8000, 400, 60, 2 → 8462	600, 7, 9000, 50 → 9657
80, 2000, 200, 4 → 2284	8000, 9, 30, 500 → 8539	70, 6, 100, 4000 → 4176

Show these numbers on the arrow cards.

- 4185 → 4000 + 100 + 80 + 5
- 6291 → 6000 + 200 + 90 + 1
- 5229 → 5000 + 200 + 20 + 9
- 6814 → 6000 + 800 + 10 + 4
- 2971 → 2000 + 900 + 70 + 1
- 9846 → 9000 + 800 + 40 + 6

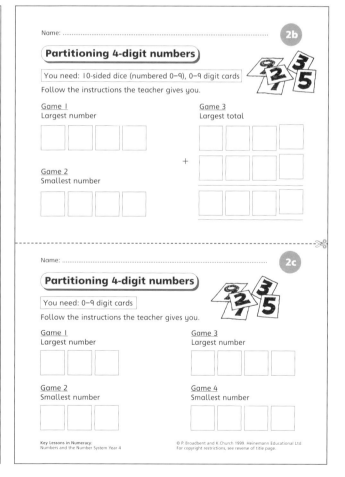

Name: **2b**

Partitioning 4-digit numbers

You need: 10-sided dice (numbered 0–9), 0–9 digit cards

Follow the instructions the teacher gives you.

Game 1
Largest number

☐☐☐☐

Game 2
Smallest number

☐☐☐☐

Game 3
Largest total

☐☐☐☐
+ ☐☐☐☐
☐☐☐☐

Name: **2c**

Partitioning 4-digit numbers

You need: 0–9 digit cards

Follow the instructions the teacher gives you.

Game 1
Largest number

☐☐☐

Game 2
Smallest number

☐☐☐

Game 3
Largest number

☐☐☐☐

Game 4
Smallest number

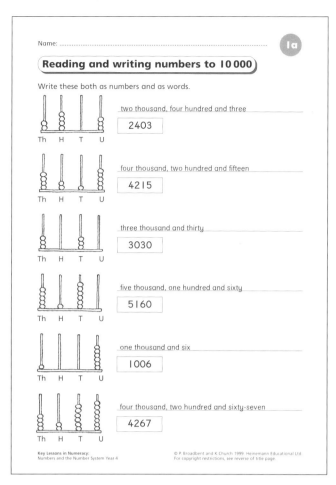

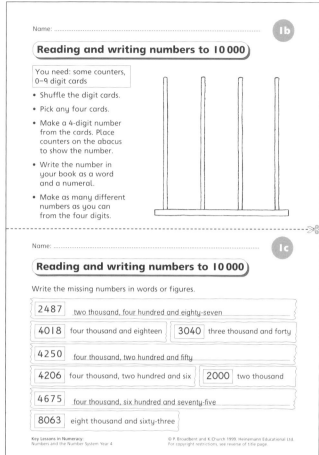

☐☐☐☐

Name: **3a**

Changing numbers by 1, 10, 100, 1000

Write the answers.

Start	+1	+10	+100	+1000
2871	2872	2881	2971	3871
6929	6930	6939	7029	7929
4198	4199	4208	4298	5198
3499	3500	3509	3599	4499

Start	−1	−10	−100	−1000
2960	2959	2950	2860	1960
4009	4008	3999	3909	3009

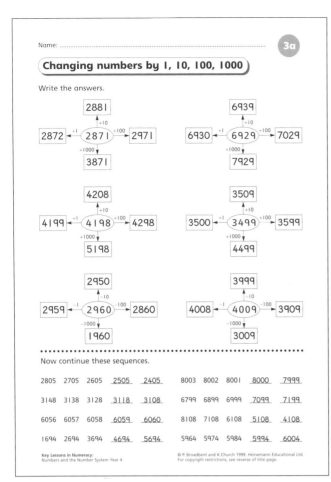

Now continue these sequences.

2805 2705 2605 2505 2405

3148 3138 3128 3118 3108

6056 6057 6058 6059 6060

1694 2694 3694 4694 5694

8003 8002 8001 8000 7999

6799 6899 6999 7099 7199

8108 7108 6108 5108 4108

5964 5974 5984 5994 6004

Name: **3b**

Changing numbers by 1, 10, 100, 1000

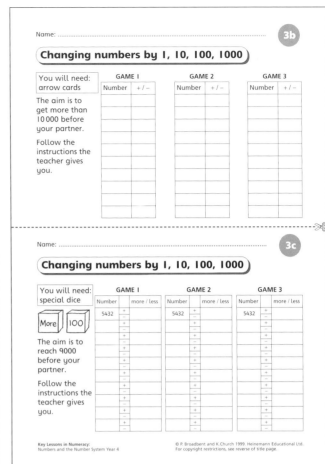

You will need: arrow cards

The aim is to get more than 10 000 before your partner.

Follow the instructions the teacher gives you.

GAME 1 Number	GAME 1 + / −	GAME 2 Number	GAME 2 + / −	GAME 3 Number	GAME 3 + / −

Name: **3c**

Changing numbers by 1, 10, 100, 1000

You will need: special dice

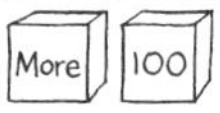

The aim is to reach 9000 before your partner.

Follow the instructions the teacher gives you.

GAME 1 Number	GAME 1 more / less	GAME 2 Number	GAME 2 more / less	GAME 3 Number	GAME 3 more / less
5432	+ / −	5432	+ / −	5432	+ / −
	+ / −		+ / −		+ / −
	+ / −		+ / −		+ / −
	+ / −		+ / −		+ / −
	+ / −		+ / −		+ / −
	+ / −		+ / −		+ / −
	+ / −		+ / −		+ / −
	+ / −		+ / −		+ / −
	+ / −		+ / −		+ / −
	+ / −		+ / −		+ / −

Name: **4a**

Multiplying and dividing by 10

Write the number shown on each abacus.
Multiply or divide the number by 10 and
draw the correct number of beads on the blank abacus.

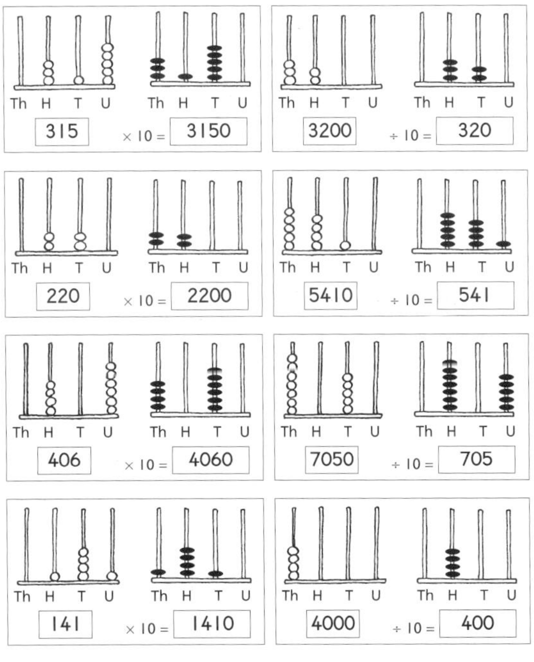

Name: **4b**

Multiplying and dividing by 10

Follow the route through the maze.
Colour the correct squares as you go.

Start → 400	×10	4000	÷10	400
×100		×10		÷10
4000	÷10	400	×100	40
÷10		×100		÷10
4	×10	40	×10	4
×10		×10		÷10
40	÷10	400	÷10	400
÷10		×100		×10
4	×10	40	×10	400 → Finish

Now make up your own maze.

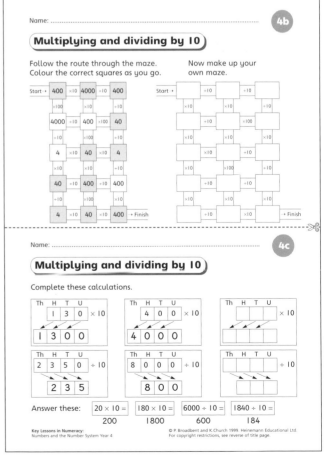

Start →	÷10		÷10	
×10		×10		÷10
	÷10		×100	
×10		×10		×10
	×10		÷10	
×10		×100		÷10
	÷10		÷10	
×10		×10		×10
	÷10		×10	→ Finish

Name: **4c**

Multiplying and dividing by 10

Complete these calculations.

Th	H	T	U	
	1	3	0	× 10
1	3	0	0	

Th	H	T	U	
	4	0	0	× 10
4	0	0	0	

Th	H	T	U	
				× 10

Th	H	T	U	
2	3	5	0	÷ 10
	2	3	5	

Th	H	T	U	
8	0	0	0	÷ 10
	8	0	0	

Th	H	T	U	
				÷ 10

Answer these: 20 × 10 = 200 | 180 × 10 = 1800 | 6000 ÷ 10 = 600 | 1840 ÷ 10 = 184

Name: **5a**

Using symbols

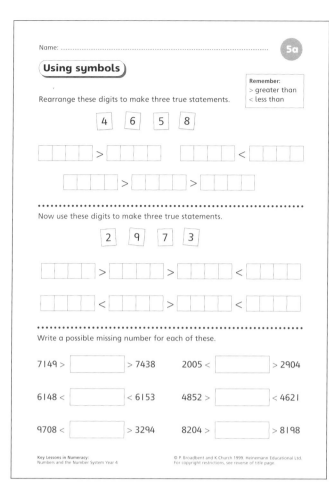

Remember:
> greater than
< less than

Rearrange these digits to make three true statements.

4 6 5 8

☐☐☐☐ > ☐☐☐☐ ☐☐☐☐ < ☐☐☐☐

☐☐☐☐ > ☐☐☐☐ > ☐☐☐☐

Now use these digits to make three true statements.

2 9 7 3

☐☐☐☐ > ☐☐☐☐ > ☐☐☐☐ < ☐☐☐☐

☐☐☐☐ < ☐☐☐☐ > ☐☐☐☐ < ☐☐☐☐

Write a possible missing number for each of these.

7149 > ☐ > 7438	2005 < ☐ > 2904
6148 < ☐ < 6153	4852 > ☐ < 4621
9708 < ☐ > 3294	8204 > ☐ > 8198

Name: **5b**

Using symbols

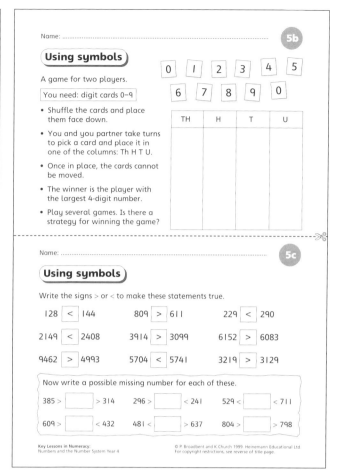

A game for two players.

You need: digit cards 0–9

0 1 2 3 4 5 6 7 8 9 0

- Shuffle the cards and place them face down.
- You and you partner take turns to pick a card and place it in one of the columns: Th H T U.
- Once in place, the cards cannot be moved.
- The winner is the player with the largest 4-digit number.
- Play several games. Is there a strategy for winning the game?

TH	H	T	U

Name: **5c**

Using symbols

Write the signs > or < to make these statements true.

128 < 144	809 > 611	229 < 290
2149 < 2408	3914 > 3099	6152 > 6083
9462 > 4993	5704 < 5741	3219 > 3129

Now write a possible missing number for each of these.

385 > ☐ > 314	296 > ☐ < 241	529 < ☐ < 711
609 > ☐ < 432	481 < ☐ > 637	804 > ☐ > 798

Name: **6a**

Comparing and ordering numbers

Write the number each arrow points to.

2000–2100: 2030, 2080	3000–4000: 3200, 3600	900–1900: 1200, 1800
5500–5600: 5520, 5550	1800–1900: 1810, 1840	6000–7000: 6300, 6800
1400–1410: 1403, 1407	2600–2700: 2620, 2670	4010–4020: 4013, 4016
2000–4000: 2400, 3400	6200–6210: 6201, 6208	1000–1100: 1040, 1060
900–1900: 1000, 1400	1500–1600: 1530, 1560	3000–5000: 3600, 4600

Write these sets of numbers in order in your books, starting with the smallest.

7250 7500 1875 5205 1780 5055
1780 1875 5055 5205 7250 7500

1085 8100 2250 2520 2025 8010
1085 2025 2250 2520 8010 8100

4100 4010 4020 1004 1240 4001
1004 1240 4001 4010 4020 4100

5105 5003 5351 5010 5315 5100
5003 5010 5100 5105 5315 5351

Name: **6b**

Comparing and ordering numbers

3 9 4 6

How many 4-digit numbers can you make from these?
Write them all in order, starting with the smallest.

3469 3496 3649 3694 3946 3964
4369 4396 4639 4693 4936 4963
6349 6394 6439 6493 6934 6943
9346 9364 9436 9463 9634 9643

Now write your own four digits. ☐ ☐ ☐ ☐

Ask a partner to write all the 4-digit numbers in order.

Name: **6c**

Comparing and ordering numbers

Write all the numbers which fit each clue.

Which numbers are greater than 255 but less than 264?
256 257 258 259 260
261 262 263

Which numbers are smaller than 1000 but greater than 985?
986 987 988 989 990
991 992 993 994 995
996 997 998 999

Which numbers come between 794 and 805?
795 796 797 798 799
800 801 802 803 804

Which numbers are greater than 1150 and smaller than 1160?
1151 1152 1153 1154 1155
1156 1157 1158 1159

Now make up some clues for your partner to answer.

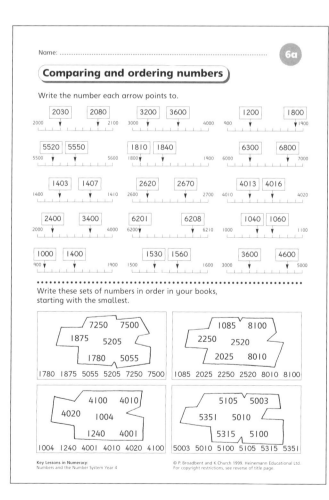

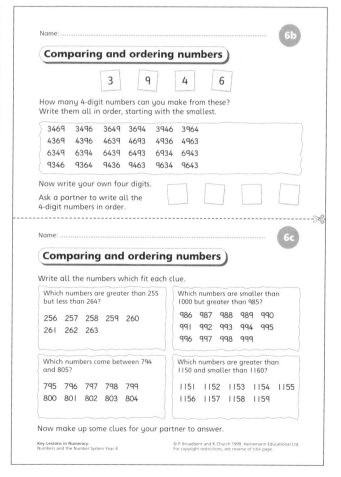

Name: **7a**

Estimation and approximation

Estimate the numbers shown by these arrows.

100, 400, 700 — number line 0 to 100

75, 200, 350 — number line 0 to 500

110, 140, 170 — number line 100 to 200

210, 240, 270 — number line 200 to 300

75, 200, 350 — number line 0 to 500

60, 90, 120 — number line 50 to 150

70, 130, 190 — number line 50 to 250

275, 350, 425 — number line 250 to 500

This jar holds 1000 sweets when it is full. Estimate the approximate number of sweets in each of these jars.

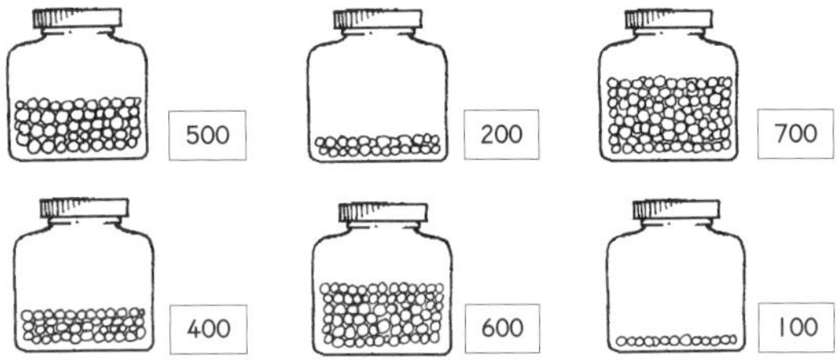

Name: **7b**

Estimation and approximation

Estimate the numbers shown by the arrows on these number lines.

30, 80 — number line 0 to 100

60, 160 — number line 0 to 200

130, 180 — number line 100 to 200

150, 400 — number line 0 to 500

530, 580 — number line 500 to 600

300, 800 — number line 0 to 1000

650, 900 — number line 500 to 1000

800, 1300 — number line 500 to 1500

3000, 8000 — number line 0 to 10 000

Estimate the position of these numbers on this number line.

752 126 317 945 63 608

63, 126, 317, 608, 752, 945 — number line 0 to 1000

Name: **7c**

Estimation and approximation

Write these sets of numbers on the number lines.
Draw an arrow to show the approximate position of the extra number.

50 85 75
25 10 60

10, 25, 50, 60, 75, 85 — number line 0 to 100

10 30 100
140 60 180

10, 30, 60, 100, 140, 180 — number line 0 to 200

250 400 300
450 100 150

100, 150, 250, 300, 400, 450 — number line 0 to 500

Name: **8a**

Rounding numbers

Round these numbers to the nearest 10 and 100.

127 — nearest 10: 130 — nearest 100: 100

342 — nearest 10: 340 — nearest 100: 300

265 — nearest 10: 270 — nearest 100: 300

406 — nearest 10: 410 — nearest 100: 400

555 — nearest 10: 560 — nearest 100: 600

351 — nearest 10: 350 — nearest 100: 400

746 — nearest 10: 750 — nearest 100: 700

838 — nearest 10: 840 — nearest 100: 800

684 — nearest 10: 680 — nearest 100: 700

Circle the best way to round the following calculations.
Write the approximate answer.

68 + 53 → 120 — (70 + 50 circled), 60 + 50, 100 + 50

47 + 86 → 140 — 40 + 80, 50 + 80, (50 + 90 circled)

95 + 42 → 140 — 100 + 50, 90 + 40, (100 + 40 circled)

83 − 46 → 30 — 80 − 40, (80 − 50 circled), 100 − 50

78 − 39 → 40 — (80 − 40 circled), 100 − 40, 70 − 40

81 × 9 → 800 — 100 × 10, (80 × 10 circled), 8 × 10

Name: **8b**

Rounding numbers

Complete this table.

Possible answers

Calculation	Rounding	Approximate answer	Higher or lower than actual answer
157 + 139	160 + 140	300	Higher
242 − 117	240 − 120	120	Lower
309 + 114	310 + 110	420	Lower
434 − 285	430 − 290	140	Lower
615 + 178	620 + 180	800	Higher
53 × 8	50 × 10	500	Higher
93 × 9	90 × 10	900	Higher
82 × 11	80 × 10	800	Lower

Name: **8c**

Rounding numbers

Round these numbers to the nearest 10. Draw a circle around your choice.

46: 40, 60, (50)

52: (50), 60, 100

84: (80), 90, 40

65: 100, 60, (70)

93: (90), 100, 95

Round these numbers to the nearest 100 and circle your choice.

128: 130, (100), 200

284: (300), 200, 290

355: 300, (400), 500

450: (500), 400, 600

349: 350, 400, (300)

Round these numbers to the nearest 10.

183 → 180   256 → 260   385 → 390   107 → 110

244 → 240   491 → 490   504 → 500   375 → 380

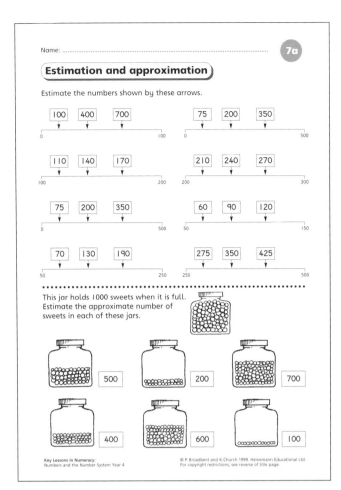

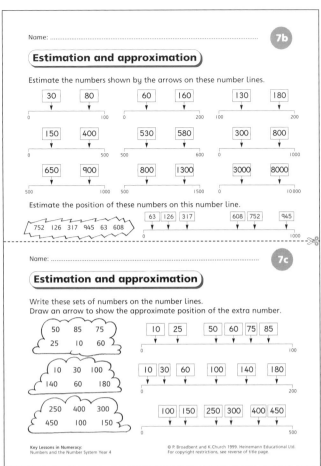

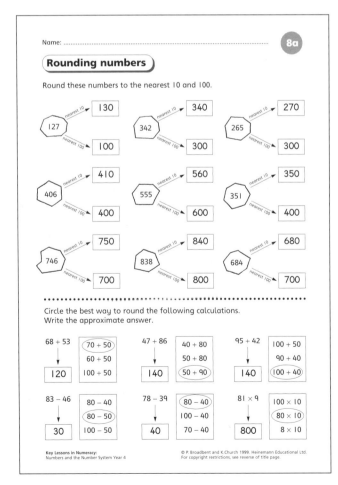

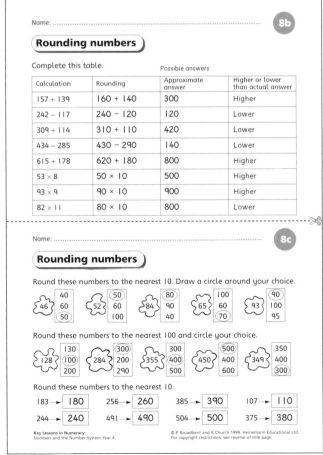

Name: 9a

Negative numbers

Write the missing numbers on these number lines.

-5 -4 -3 -2 -1 0 1 2 3 4 5

-9 -8 -7 -6 -5 -4 -3 -2 -1 0 1 2 3 4 5

-9 -8 -7 -6 -5 -4 -3 -2 -1 0 1 2 3 4 5 6 7 8

Continue the patterns on these number lines.
Write the numbers that the penguin lands on.

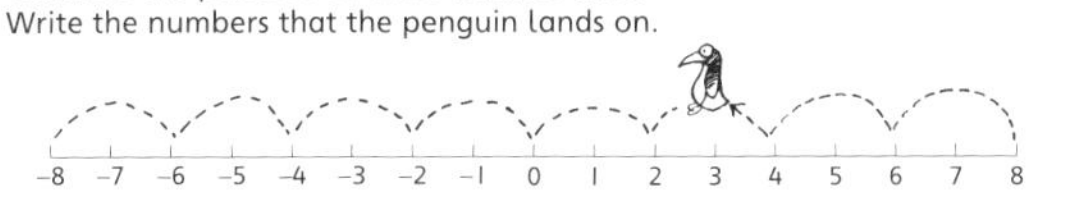

8 6 4 2 0 -2 -4 -6 -8

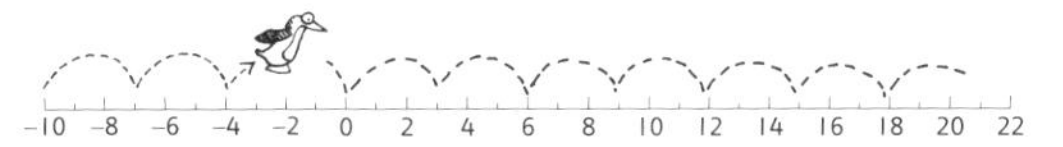

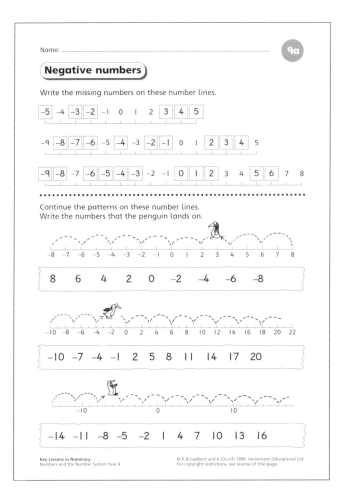

-10 -7 -4 -1 2 5 8 11 14 17 20

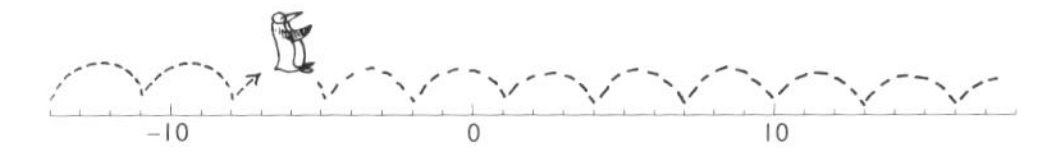

-14 -11 -8 -5 -2 1 4 7 10 13 16

Key Lessons in Numeracy:
Numbers and the Number System Year 4

Name: 9b

Negative numbers

Copy and complete these number sequences.
Write the rule for each sequence in your book.

1.	-6	-4	-2	0	2	4	6	8	add 2
2.	-12	-9	-6	-3	0	3	6	9	add 3
3.	-7	-5	-3	-1	1	3	5	7	add 2
4.	-12	-8	-4	0	4	8	12	16	add 4
5.	-10	-7	-4	-1	2	5	8	11	add 3

Now make up five more negative number sequences and write them in your book.

Name: 9c

Negative numbers

Write the temperatures shown on these thermometers.

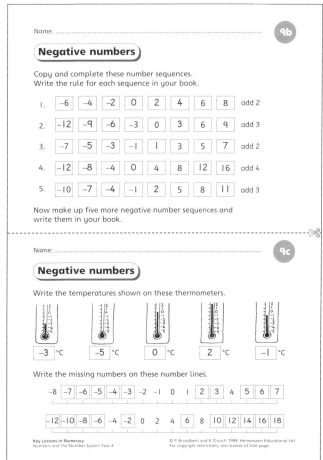

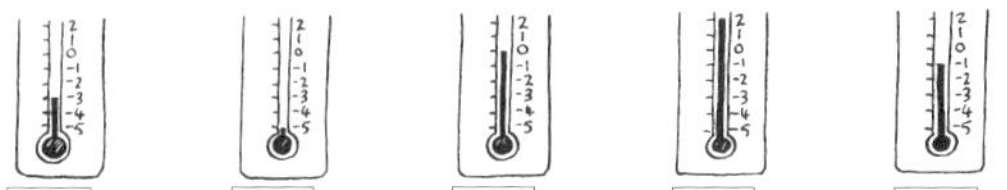

-3 °C, -5 °C, 0 °C, 2 °C, -1 °C

Write the missing numbers on these number lines.

-8 -7 -6 -5 -4 -3 -2 -1 0 1 2 3 4 5 6 7

-12 -10 -8 -6 -4 -2 0 2 4 6 8 10 12 14 16 18

Key Lessons in Numeracy:
Numbers and the Number System Year 4

Name: 10a

Number sequences

Continue these sequences and write the rule for each one.

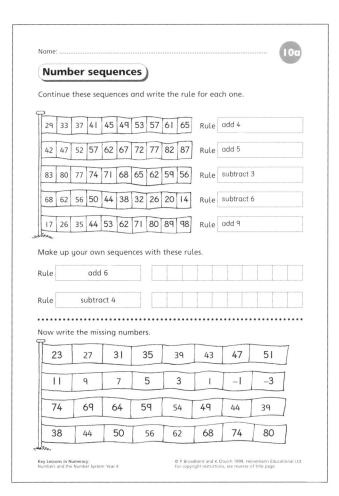

29	33	37	41	45	49	53	57	61	65	Rule	add 4
42	47	52	57	62	67	72	77	82	87	Rule	add 5
83	80	77	74	71	68	65	62	59	56	Rule	subtract 3
68	62	56	50	44	38	32	26	20	14	Rule	subtract 6
17	26	35	44	53	62	71	80	89	98	Rule	add 9

Make up your own sequences with these rules.

Rule add 6

Rule subtract 4

Now write the missing numbers.

23	27	31	35	39	43	47	51
11	9	7	5	3	1	-1	-3
74	69	64	59	54	49	44	39
38	44	50	56	62	68	74	80

Key Lessons in Numeracy:
Numbers and the Number System Year 4

Name: 10b

Number sequences

You will need: Number Grid 1

- Count on in fours from 0, colouring in the numbers, so it begins 3, 7...
  What pattern do you notice?
- Count on in fours on the other five grids.
  What patterns do you notice?
- Use different colours to show counting on in threes and fives on all six grids.
- Describe your patterns.

Name: 10c

Number sequences

Record your sequences here.

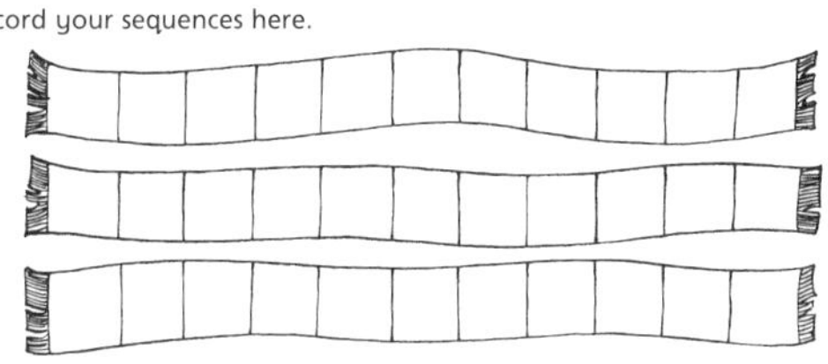

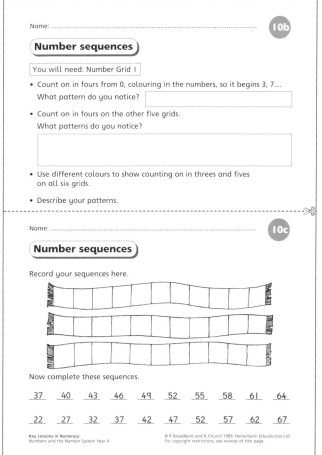

Now complete these sequences.

37 40 43 46 49 52 55 58 61 64

22 27 32 37 42 47 52 57 62 67

Key Lessons in Numeracy:
Numbers and the Number System Year 4

Name: ....

11a

Odds and evens

Write the missing numbers in these sequences.

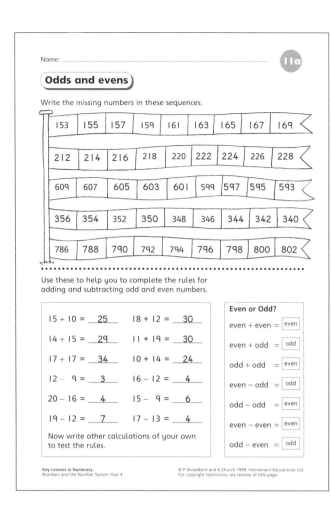

153	155	157	159	161	163	165	167	169
212	214	216	218	220	222	224	226	228
609	607	605	603	601	599	597	595	593
356	354	352	350	348	346	344	342	340
786	788	790	792	794	796	798	800	802

Use these to help you to complete the rules for adding and subtracting odd and even numbers.

15 + 10 = 25 18 + 12 = 30

14 + 15 = 29 11 + 19 = 30

17 + 17 = 34 10 + 14 = 24

12 – 9 = 3 16 – 12 = 4

20 – 16 = 4 15 – 9 = 6

19 – 12 = 7 17 – 13 = 4

Now write other calculations of your own to test the rules.

Even or Odd?

even + even = even

even + odd = odd

odd + odd = even

even – odd = odd

odd – odd = even

even – even = even

odd – even = odd

Name: ....

11b

Odds and evens

You are going to investigate consecutive numbers.

- Do you get an odd or an even total when you add two consecutive numbers? Why? odd, because odd + even = odd
- What about when you add three consecutive numbers? if the first number is odd: odd + even + odd = even
  if the first number is even: even + odd + even = odd
- Or four consecutive numbers? even

Record your results and explain any patterns you find in your book.

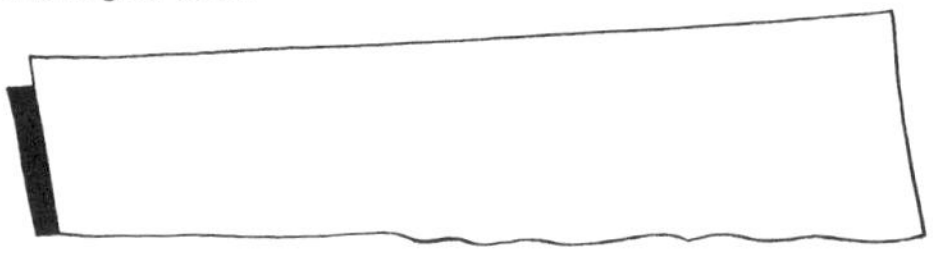

Name: ....

11c

Odds and evens

Write these numbers in the correct set.

Odd numbers	Even numbers
end in 1, 3, 5, 7, 9	end in 0, 2, 4, 6, 8
27 51 77 43 45	38 46 86 80 84 78 30 94 28 72 34

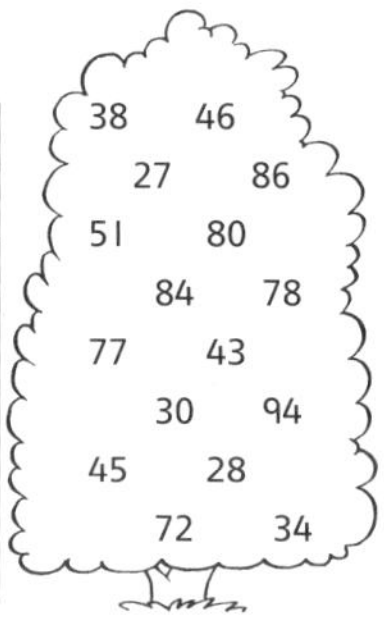

Name: ....

12a

Recognizing multiples

Look at this multiple tree diagram.
Put each number through it to see where it ends up.

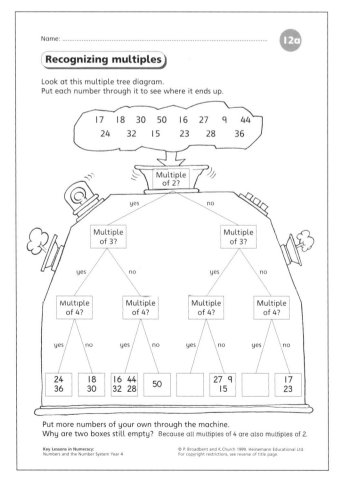

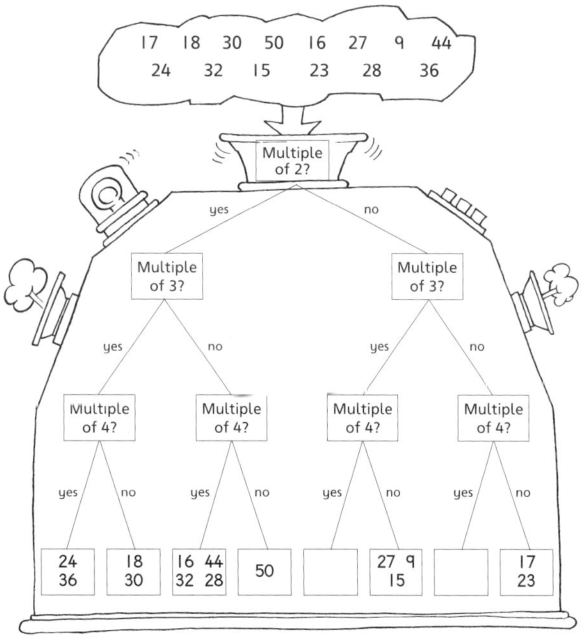

Put more numbers of your own through the machine.
Why are two boxes still empty? Because all multiples of 4 are also multiples of 2.

Name: ....

12b

Recognizing multiples

Circle the odd one out in each set.
Write why each number is the odd one out.

38 84 46 70 (83) 92 not a multiple of 2

(53) 60 69 72 87 45 not a multiple of 3

(45) 70 100 90 120 60 not a multiple of 10

80 92 96 64 (54) 76 not a multiple of 4

800 400 700 200 (550) 900 not a multiple of 100

75 95 80 35 40 (64) not a multiple of 5

138 108 114 180 160 (153) not a multiple of 2 or (160) not a multiple of 3

150 300 500 (605) 100 450 not a multiple of 50

Name: ....

12c

Recognizing multiples

In the 1–100 square:

- Colour the multiples of 2 yellow.
- Circle the multiples of 3 in blue.
- Cross out the multiples of 4.

What patterns do you notice?

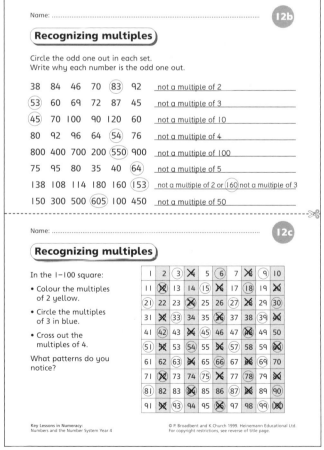

1	2	3	4	5	6	7	8	9	10
11	12	13	14	15	16	17	18	19	20
21	22	23	24	25	26	27	28	29	30
31	32	33	34	35	36	37	38	39	40
41	42	43	44	45	46	47	48	49	50
51	52	53	54	55	56	57	58	59	60
61	62	63	64	65	66	67	68	69	70
71	72	73	74	75	76	77	78	79	80
81	82	83	84	85	86	87	88	89	90
91	92	93	94	95	96	97	98	99	100

Name: **13a**

Non-unitary fractions

Colour $\frac{3}{4}$ of each shape.

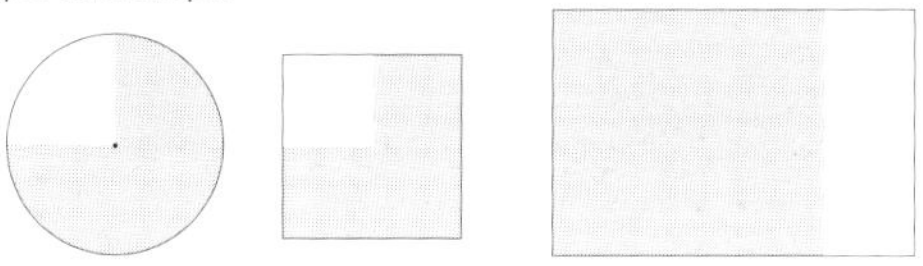

Colour $\frac{2}{3}$ of each shape.

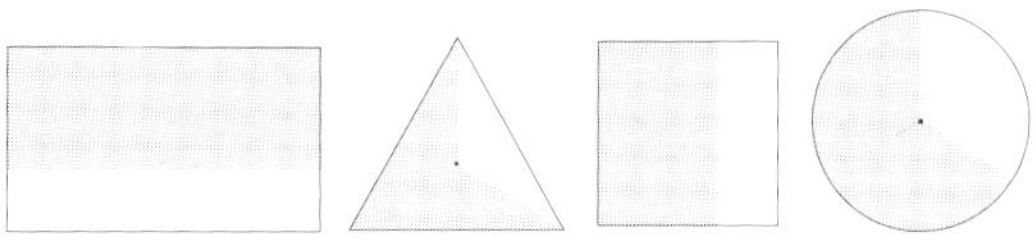

Colour $\frac{3}{5}$ of each shape.

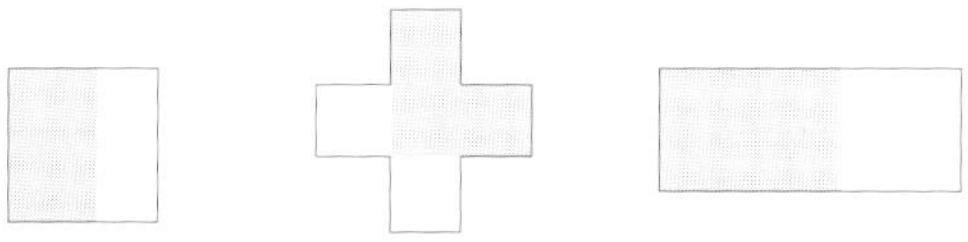

Colour $\frac{7}{8}$ of each shape.

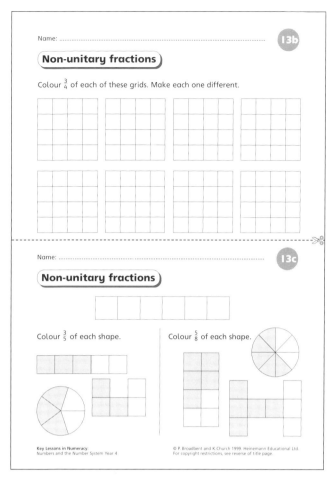

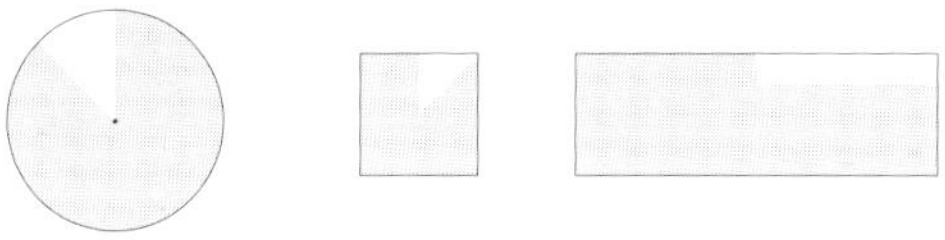

Name: **13b**

Non-unitary fractions

Colour $\frac{3}{4}$ of each of these grids. Make each one different.

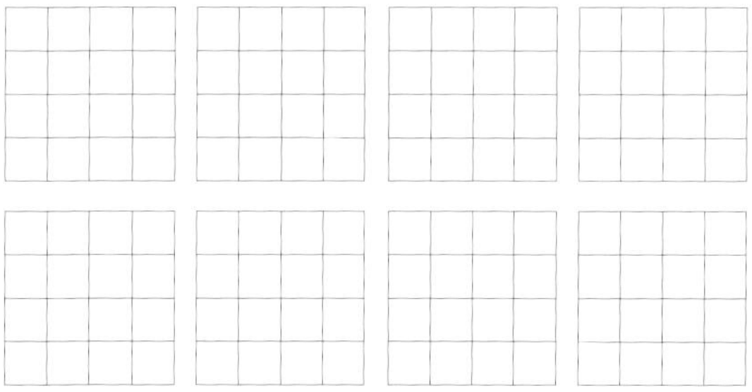

Name: **13c**

Non-unitary fractions

Colour $\frac{3}{5}$ of each shape.

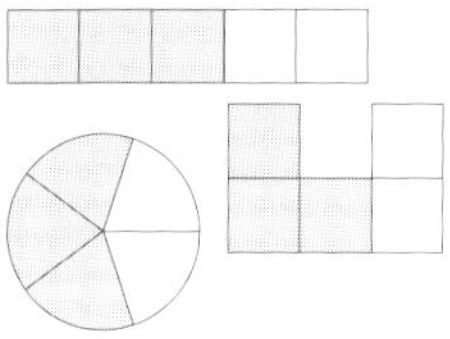

Colour $\frac{5}{8}$ of each shape.

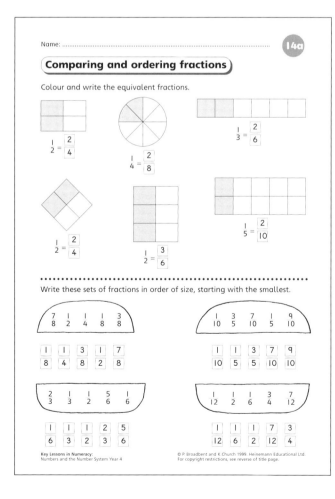

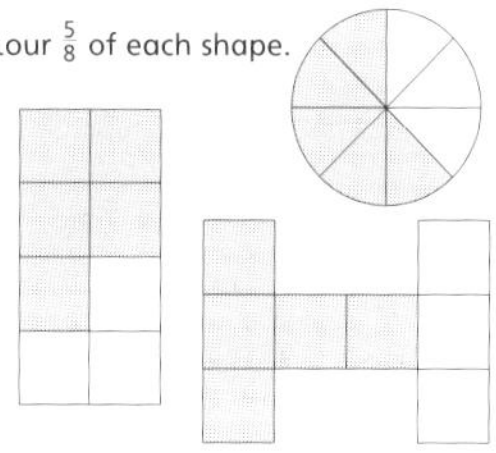

Name: **14a**

Comparing and ordering fractions

Colour and write the equivalent fractions.

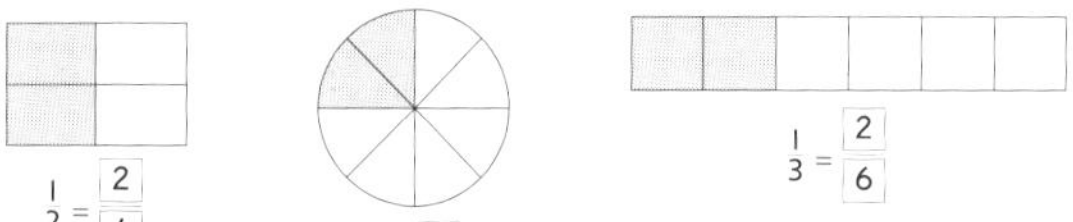

$\frac{1}{2} = \frac{2}{4}$ $\frac{1}{4} = \frac{2}{8}$ $\frac{1}{3} = \frac{2}{6}$

$\frac{1}{2} = \frac{2}{4}$ $\frac{1}{2} = \frac{3}{6}$ $\frac{1}{5} = \frac{2}{10}$

Write these sets of fractions in order of size, starting with the smallest.

$\frac{7}{8}$ $\frac{1}{2}$ $\frac{1}{4}$ $\frac{1}{8}$ $\frac{3}{8}$

$\frac{1}{8}$ $\frac{1}{4}$ $\frac{3}{8}$ $\frac{1}{2}$ $\frac{7}{8}$

$\frac{1}{10}$ $\frac{3}{5}$ $\frac{7}{10}$ $\frac{1}{5}$ $\frac{9}{10}$

$\frac{1}{10}$ $\frac{1}{5}$ $\frac{3}{5}$ $\frac{7}{10}$ $\frac{9}{10}$

$\frac{2}{3}$ $\frac{1}{3}$ $\frac{1}{2}$ $\frac{5}{6}$ $\frac{1}{6}$

$\frac{1}{6}$ $\frac{1}{3}$ $\frac{1}{2}$ $\frac{2}{3}$ $\frac{5}{6}$

$\frac{1}{12}$ $\frac{1}{2}$ $\frac{1}{6}$ $\frac{3}{4}$ $\frac{7}{12}$

$\frac{1}{12}$ $\frac{1}{6}$ $\frac{1}{2}$ $\frac{7}{12}$ $\frac{3}{4}$

Name: **14b**

Comparing and ordering fractions

- Use these numbers to make fractions.
- Each fraction must be less than 1.
- Write the fractions in order, starting with the smallest.

1 3 8 10 2 4 5 6

$\frac{1}{10}, \frac{1}{8}, \frac{1}{6}, \frac{2}{10} = \frac{1}{5}, \frac{2}{8} = \frac{1}{4}, \frac{3}{10}, \frac{2}{6} = \frac{1}{3}, \frac{3}{8}, \frac{4}{10} = \frac{2}{5},$

$\frac{5}{10} = \frac{4}{8} = \frac{3}{6} = \frac{2}{4} = \frac{1}{2}, \frac{6}{10} = \frac{3}{5}, \frac{5}{8}, \frac{4}{6} = \frac{2}{3}, \frac{6}{8} = \frac{3}{4}, \frac{8}{10} = \frac{4}{5}, \frac{5}{6}$

Name: **14c**

Comparing and ordering fractions

Compare these fractions.

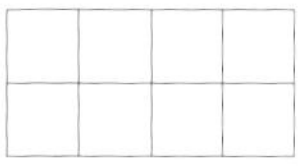

$\frac{1}{2}$ $\frac{1}{4}$ $\frac{1}{8}$

Smallest — Largest

$\frac{1}{8}$ $\frac{1}{4}$ $\frac{1}{2}$

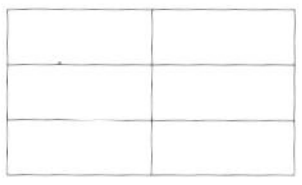

$\frac{1}{2}$ $\frac{1}{6}$ $\frac{1}{3}$

Smallest — Largest

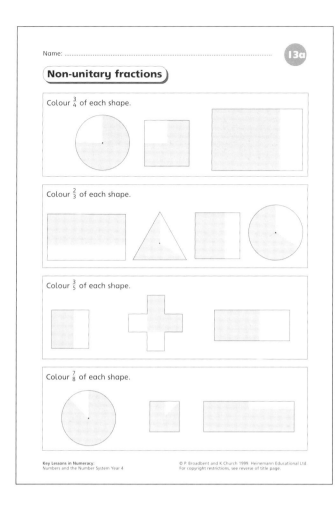

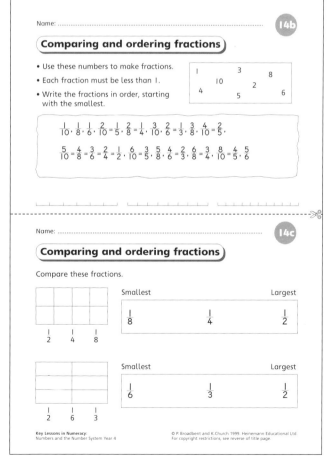

$\frac{1}{6}$ $\frac{1}{3}$ $\frac{1}{2}$

Name: ....

15a

Fractions totalling one

Draw lines to show the missing fractions.
Write the fractions so that the total is 1.

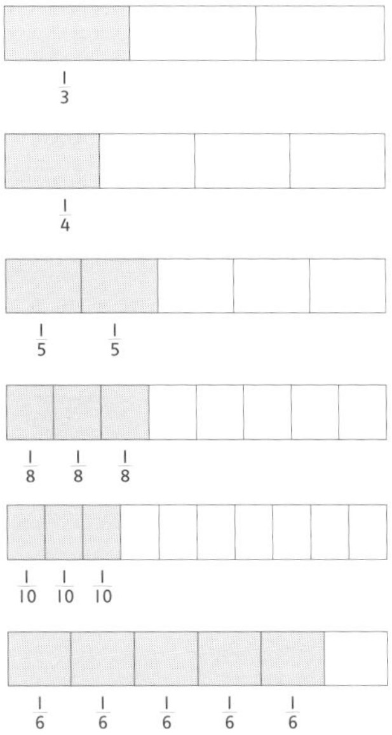

$\frac{1}{3} + \boxed{\frac{2}{3}} = 1$

$\frac{1}{4} + \boxed{\frac{3}{4}} = 1$

$\frac{2}{5} + \boxed{\frac{3}{5}} = 1$

$\frac{3}{8} + \boxed{\frac{5}{8}} = 1$

$\frac{3}{10} + \boxed{\frac{7}{10}} = 1$

$\frac{5}{6} + \boxed{\frac{1}{6}} = 1$

Draw a diagram to show that $\frac{7}{12} + \frac{5}{12} = 1$

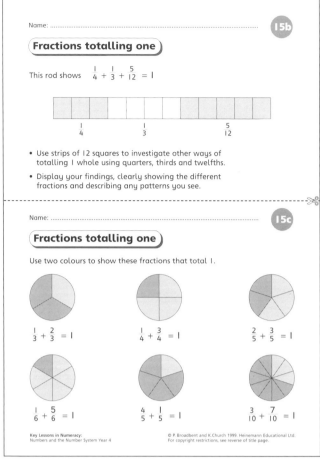

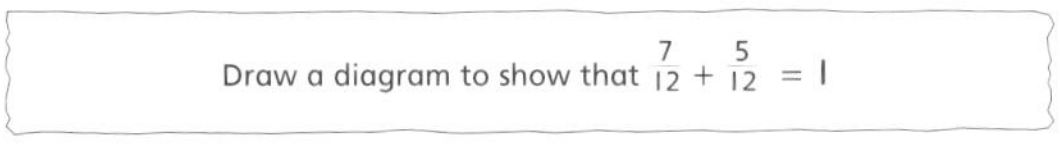

Key Lessons in Numeracy:
Numbers and the Number System Year 4

Name: ....

15b

Fractions totalling one

This rod shows $\frac{1}{4} + \frac{1}{3} + \frac{5}{12} = 1$

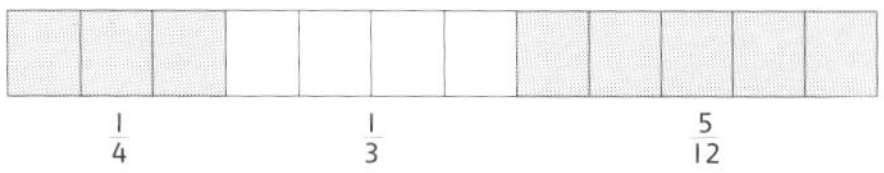

- Use strips of 12 squares to investigate other ways of totalling 1 whole using quarters, thirds and twelfths.
- Display your findings, clearly showing the different fractions and describing any patterns you see.

Name: ....

15c

Fractions totalling one

Use two colours to show these fractions that total 1.

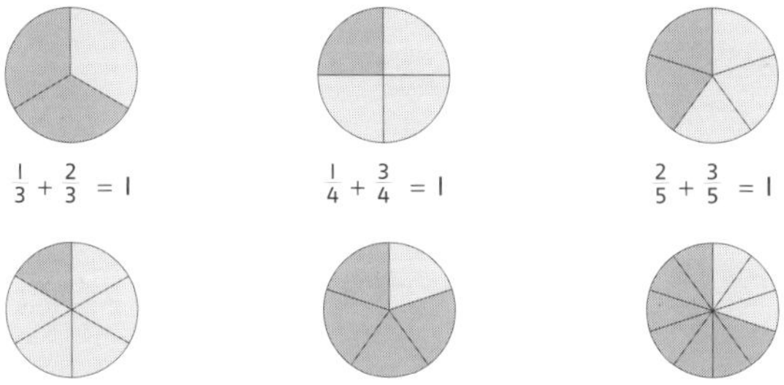

$\frac{1}{3} + \frac{2}{3} = 1$ $\frac{1}{4} + \frac{3}{4} = 1$ $\frac{2}{5} + \frac{3}{5} = 1$

$\frac{1}{6} + \frac{5}{6} = 1$ $\frac{4}{5} + \frac{1}{5} = 1$ $\frac{3}{10} + \frac{7}{10} = 1$

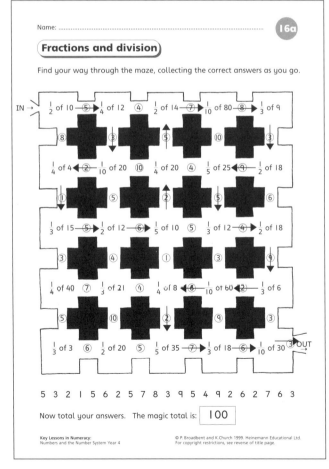

Key Lessons in Numeracy:
Numbers and the Number System Year 4

Name: ....

16a

Fractions and division

Find your way through the maze, collecting the correct answers as you go.

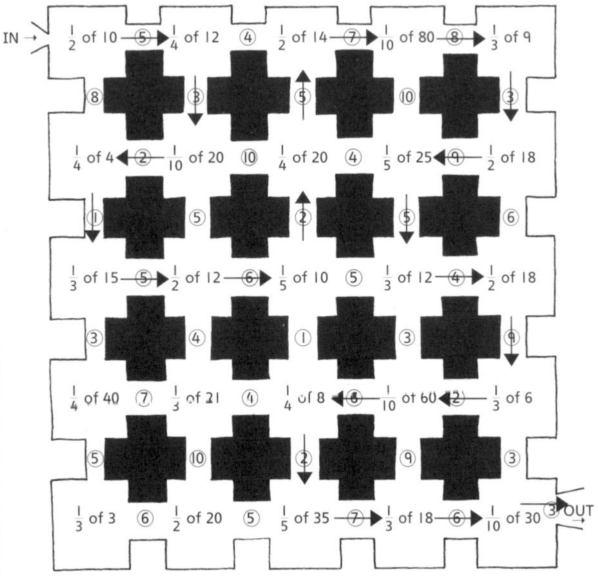

5 3 2 1 5 6 2 5 7 8 3 9 5 4 9 2 6 2 7 6 3

Now total your answers. The magic total is: **100**

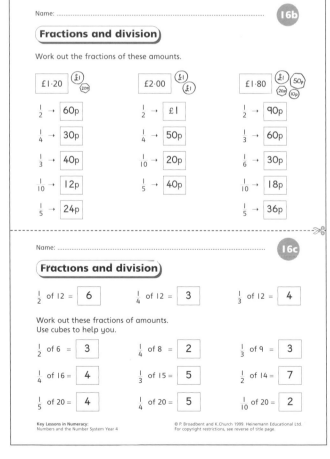

Key Lessons in Numeracy:
Numbers and the Number System Year 4

Name: ....

16b

Fractions and division

Work out the fractions of these amounts.

£1·20	£2·00	£1·80
$\frac{1}{2}$ → 60p	$\frac{1}{2}$ → £1	$\frac{1}{2}$ → 90p
$\frac{1}{4}$ → 30p	$\frac{1}{4}$ → 50p	$\frac{1}{3}$ → 60p
$\frac{1}{3}$ → 40p	$\frac{1}{10}$ → 20p	$\frac{1}{6}$ → 30p
$\frac{1}{10}$ → 12p	$\frac{1}{5}$ → 40p	$\frac{1}{10}$ → 18p
$\frac{1}{5}$ → 24p		$\frac{1}{5}$ → 36p

Name: ....

16c

Fractions and division

$\frac{1}{2}$ of 12 = 6 $\frac{1}{4}$ of 12 = 3 $\frac{1}{3}$ of 12 = 4

Work out these fractions of amounts.
Use cubes to help you.

$\frac{1}{2}$ of 6 = 3 $\frac{1}{4}$ of 8 = 2 $\frac{1}{3}$ of 9 = 3

$\frac{1}{4}$ of 16 = 4 $\frac{1}{3}$ of 15 = 5 $\frac{1}{2}$ of 14 = 7

$\frac{1}{5}$ of 20 = 4 $\frac{1}{4}$ of 20 = 5 $\frac{1}{10}$ of 20 = 2

Key Lessons in Numeracy:
Numbers and the Number System Year 4

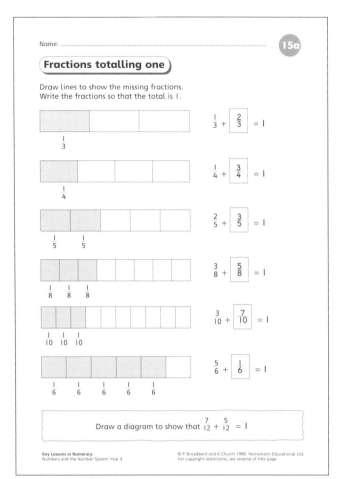

Name: ....

17a

Simple proportion

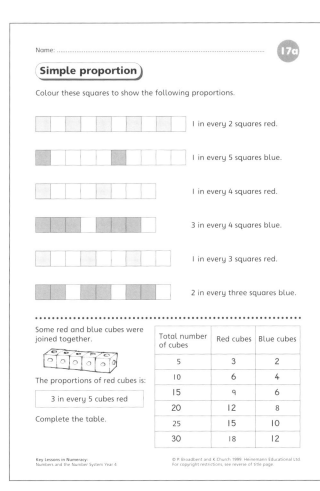

Colour these squares to show the following proportions.

I in every 2 squares red.

I in every 5 squares blue.

I in every 4 squares red.

3 in every 4 squares blue.

I in every 3 squares red.

2 in every three squares blue.

Some red and blue cubes were joined together.

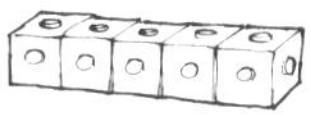

The proportions of red cubes is:

3 in every 5 cubes red

Complete the table.

Total number of cubes	Red cubes	Blue cubes
5	3	2
10	6	4
15	9	6
20	12	8
25	15	10
30	18	12

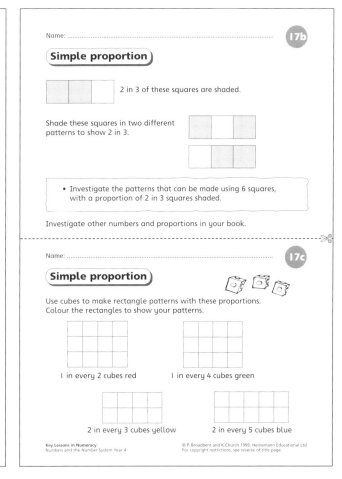

Name: ....

17b

Simple proportion

2 in 3 of these squares are shaded.

Shade these squares in two different patterns to show 2 in 3.

- Investigate the patterns that can be made using 6 squares, with a proportion of 2 in 3 squares shaded.

Investigate other numbers and proportions in your book.

Name: ....

17c

Simple proportion

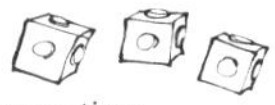

Use cubes to make rectangle patterns with these proportions.
Colour the rectangles to show your patterns.

I in every 2 cubes red

I in every 4 cubes green

2 in every 3 cubes yellow

2 in every 5 cubes blue

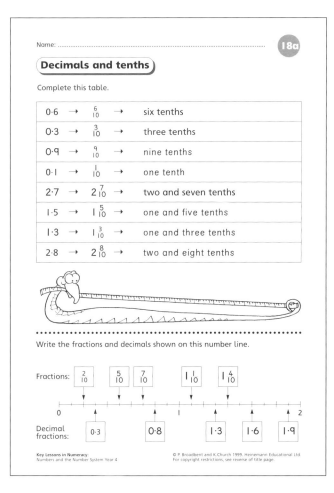

Name: ....

18a

Decimals and tenths

Complete this table.

0·6	→	$\frac{6}{10}$	→	six tenths
0·3	→	$\frac{3}{10}$	→	three tenths
0·9	→	$\frac{9}{10}$	→	nine tenths
0·1	→	$\frac{1}{10}$	→	one tenth
2·7	→	$2\frac{7}{10}$	→	two and seven tenths
1·5	→	$1\frac{5}{10}$	→	one and five tenths
1·3	→	$1\frac{3}{10}$	→	one and three tenths
2·8	→	$2\frac{8}{10}$	→	two and eight tenths

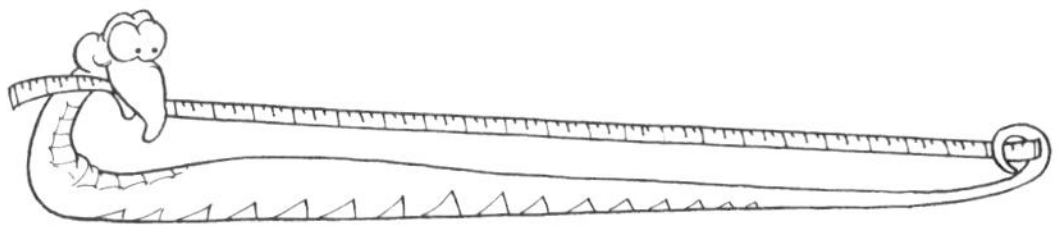

Write the fractions and decimals shown on this number line.

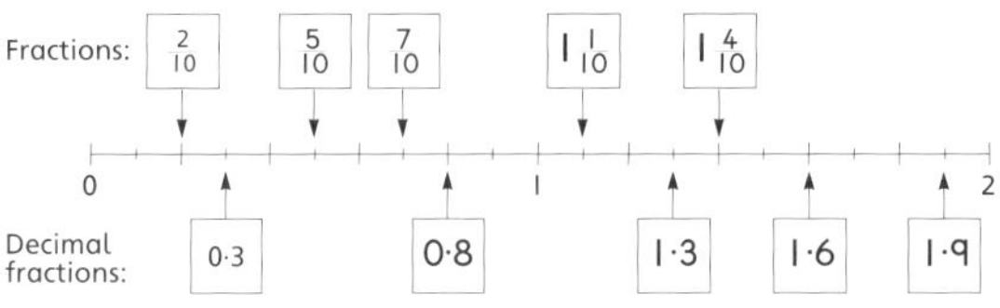

Name: ....

18b

Decimals and tenths

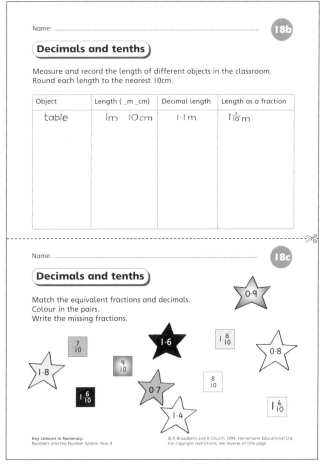

Measure and record the length of different objects in the classroom.
Round each length to the nearest 10cm.

Object	Length (_m _cm)	Decimal length	Length as a fraction
table	1m 10cm	1·1m	$1\frac{1}{10}$m

Name: ....

18c

Decimals and tenths

Match the equivalent fractions and decimals.
Colour in the pairs.
Write the missing fractions.

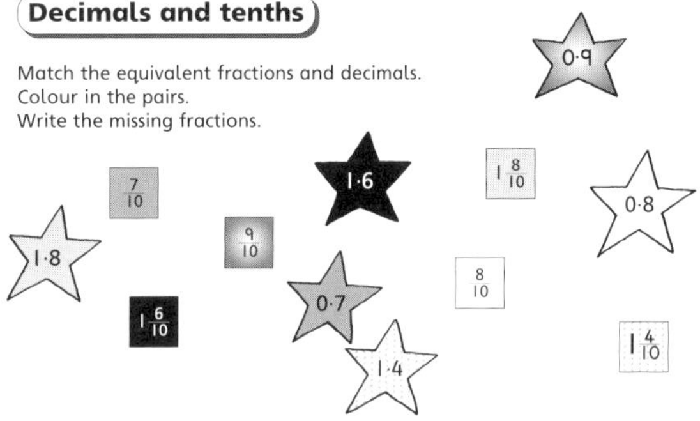

Name: 19a

Decimals and money

bread	£0·65
butter	£1·03
orange juice	£2·59
cheese	£4·66
toilet roll	£3·97
sausages	£2·72
ham	£3·18
milk	£0·89
Total	£19·69
Received	£20·00
Change	£0·31

Use the receipt to answer these questions in your book.

1. Which is the most expensive item? *cheese*
2. Which items are between 50p and £1? *bread and milk*
3. Which item costs 103p? *butter*
4. Which item is nearest in price to £4? *toilet roll*
5. How much does the bread and butter cost together? *£1·68*
6. How much change will be given from £20? *31p*

sticky tape	£0·76
paperclips	£0·92
5 pencils	£1·08
glue	£1·27
ink pen	£2·19
writing paper	£2·45
4 folders	£3·33
envelopes	£4·63
Total	£16·63

Use this blank receipt to write the following prices in order, starting with the lowest price.

sticky tape £0·76
5 pencils £1·08
glue £1·27
envelopes £4·63
writing paper £2·45
paperclips £0·92
ink pen £2·19
4 folders £3·33

Key Lessons in Numeracy: Numbers and the Number System Year 4

Name: 19b

Decimals and money

- The digits 1 6 5 can make £1·65. They can also make £6·15, £1·56, £5·61, and so on.
- If the rule is that the decimal point always comes after the first digit, which other numbers can be made?

£5·16 and £6·51

- Using the same rule, investigate all the amounts that can be made from 4 2 7

Remember, the rule is that the decimal point comes after the first digit.

Write the amounts in order in your book. *£2·47 £4·27 £7·24 £2·74 £4·72 £7·42*

Name: 19c

Decimals and money

Write these as decimal money.

example: 485p → £4·85

140p →	£1·40	225p →	£2·25	308p →	£3·08
250p →	£2·50	380p →	£3·80	219p →	£2·19
85p →	£0·85	104p →	£1·04	195p →	£1·95
200p →	£2	231p →	£2·31	205p →	£2·05

Now write these amounts in order, starting with the lowest price.

£0·85, £1·04, £1·40, £1·95, £2, £2·05, £2·19, £2·25, £2·31, £2·50, £3·08, £3·80

Key Lessons in Numeracy: Numbers and the Number System Year 4

Name: 20a

Rounding decimals

yoghurt	£1·09
soup	£0·75
washing powder	£4·81
soap	£1·55
toothpaste	£2·87
apples	£1·47
cheese	£3·80
lemonade	£1·70
pizza	£4·19
tomatoes	£1·40
Total	

Use the receipt to answer these questions.

1. Which item costs approximately £5? *washing powder*
2. What is the approximate price of the toothpaste? *£3*
3. What is the approximate total of the pizza and the lemonade? *£6*
4. What is the approximate price of the yoghurt? *£1*

I think the bill is about £28.

Now choose some of the items on the receipt to make an approximate total of £10.

5. Is Mr Harris correct? Work out the approximate total for the shopping bill. *£24*

Key Lessons in Numeracy: Numbers and the Number System Year 4

Name: 20b

Rounding decimals

You will need: a shopping catalogue

- Choose ten items from the catalogue and list them.
- Round each price to the nearest pound.
- What is your total? Your total approximate price must not go over £100.

How close to £100 can you get?

Name: 20c

Rounding decimals

Round these amounts to the nearest £ (pound).

example: £1·20 → £1

£1·80 →	£2	£4·25 →	£4	£2·60 →	£3
£3·55 →	£4	£5·09 →	£5	£3·50 →	£4
£4·49 →	£4	£2·62 →	£3	£2·01 →	£2
£5·69 →	£6	£1·51 →	£2	£3·39 →	£3

Key Lessons in Numeracy: Numbers and the Number System Year 4

Running for a Fry

Thomas Gideon Stove

Running for a Fry

AND OTHER SHETLAND FIDDLE TUNES

Thomas Gideon Stove

Running for a Fry

ISBN 1 904746 10 1

First published by The Shetland Times Ltd., 2005

British Library Cataloguing-in-Publication Data
A catalogue record for this book is available from the British Library.

Front cover photo: Landing herring, Peterhead.

Printed and published by
The Shetland Times Ltd.,
Gremista, Lerwick
Shetland ZE1 0PX, UK.

Contents

Foreword

AS A YOUNG FIDDLER growing up in rural Aberdeenshire there were probably five players who really inspired me. My teacher Douglas Lawrence, the legendary Hector MacAndrew, Angus Cameron, Aly Bain and Willie Hunter. It is interesting to note that two of my favourite players are Shetlanders and it is probably as good an example as any to highlight the influence that the Shetland Isles have had on fiddle music, not just in Scotland but worldwide.

Every year musicians from all corners of the globe arrive in Shetland to perform at the various festivals and I'm sure many feel much as I did on my first visit to the fiddle and accordion festival in 1991, excitement with a touch of nervousness. You see there was one thing I knew about Shetlanders – they know fiddle music!

On that first trip to the fiddle and accordion festival I was staying with the 'weel kent' figure of Henry Henderson, and during the weekend he gifted me a collection of compositions by Gideon Stove. Though I knew the 'Guizers March' I had to admit I had never heard of Gideon Stove, so it was of great interest to hear of the huge impact he'd had on the artistic life of Shetland. He had been invited to play with the London Philharmonic but even more importantly he had taught Arthur Scot Robertson and Willie Hunter! So fourteen years later it is with great pleasure that I introduce the compositions of Gideon's grandson, Thomas Stove.

Thomas, a native of Shetland though now living in the north east, writes with a natural instinct for composition and I feel sure that this, his first collection of fiddle music, will stand the test of time and become an important part of Shetland's fiddle tradition. Gideon would have been proud!

Paul Anderson

Introduction

WELCOME TO THIS COLLECTION of traditional tunes composed, played and arranged by myself, with the skilled accompaniment of Liz Slaven, who with the recording skill of her husband, started this whole project off in the first place. John, a fair fiddler in his own right, came to me for some lessons and, on hearing me play some bits and pieces, asked why I had never published anything. I must admit I had been asked but usually just put it down to people trying to be nice. I never thought any publisher would take me seriously. Anyway, John persisted and said he would get me a publisher himself if I didn't. I was still sceptical but one day, while doing a bit of practice and mulling over what had been said, I thought what harm can it do to ask someone. So I phoned The Shetland Times and was told by Mrs Charlotte Black, yes we are interested, send them up!

The Shetland Folk Society published a book of my grandfather Gideon Stove's tunes in 1986 edited by my uncle Magnus James, saving at least some of the hundreds of tunes written by my grandfather from being lost and forgotten forever. I suppose this has been the fate of many a good tune and even whole tune collections over the ages. Mine might easily have gone the same way but for the help of The Shetland Times and John Slaven. Lets hope they are worth saving.

When I first picked up the fiddle at the age of about thirteen I was considered too old to start playing. Now at fifty-two I suppose some would say I am too old to start recording a CD. These are probably the same people who told me that my treasured Sean Maguire records were too avant-garde and not proper traditional music. My first ever record purchased was the LP Sean Maguire Plays priced 12/6d from the Music Box, Lerwick. I played that record until I think it wore away, so it is with a sad heart that I write this now having just heard of his passing. He will always be remembered as having influenced many traditional artists not only in Ireland and Scotland but worldwide.

Along with the influence of Sean Maguire, I had the luxury and misfortune to come from a musical family. This can work both ways – it can be an advantage, or very frustrating. I can remember when I was young playing my heart out one afternoon in the Lounge Bar and being the centre of attention, "great boy, great, whits de name?" Stove! If I had said any name but Stove I would have been a great player, but my family were notorious in Shetland for their music making so it was just a case of, "he's wan o da Stoves!"

The late Ronald Cooper was the first Shetland artist outside the family to make an impression on me. Like most youngsters I discovered pubs, and inevitably The Lounge musical events on Saturday night, and best of all, Saturday afternoon. The feeling of turning the corner at the Market Cross to hear Ronnie Cooper's accordion is unforgettable, the music seemed to pull my feet along up the lane into musical heaven. There was always a selection of locals willing to join Ronnie on piano, second accordion, fiddle, guitar, double bass etc, and he was always keen to give a budding musician a chance. There must be hundreds of Shetlanders and visitors alike who can say they had a tune with Ronald Cooper, a true gentleman and a greatly admired musician and composer.

Willie Hunter was a visitor to The Lounge occasionally and I suppose that must be where I first got friendly with him. He was always giving me advice and encouraging me to take the fiddle more seriously. I liked talking to Willie as he would start reminiscing about my grandfather Gideon, telling me about how he went to him for lessons when he was young. Unfortunately I never knew Gideon as he died when I was only one year old, so hearing Willie's stories filled in a lot of details I was unaware of. I can remember someone on the pier one day talking to me about fiddlers and asking who I thought was the best fiddler. I said Willie Hunter is not only the best in Shetland he's one of the best in Scotland. I was shot down in flames and laughed at. I decided maybe I was a bit bias as Willie was a friend and fellow Shetlander. I don't think anyone would laugh or disagree now. The last time I met Willie was just before he died. He was as usual full of advice for me and it's partly due to his advice that I decided to go to Aberdeen Music College.

This introduction would not be complete if Willie Johnson or Peerie Willie as he is known was left out. I met Willie when I was about 16 and worked for Jock Lawrie. It was part of my job to go over with the van driver to the HIB fish factory where Willie was mostly working in the freezers. Anyone who knows him will know that Willie is the kind who always has a smile on his face and likes a good yarn. As soon as he found out who I was he was telling me all about his jazz playing days in Aberdeen and his escapades with my father at Sullom Voe when they were in the RAF. Willie was often to be found accompanying Ronald Cooper on his old guitar, although I have seen him playing piano, double bass, and I can remember him playing me a tune on the fiddle once. There's no doubt that Willie has even more strings to his bow, but one thing I am sure of when I encounter Willie is a smile and a warm welcome.

If you asked me to name a favourite tune from this collection I would find it very difficult indeed because they all bring back memories or reminders of someone. Dollar's Box is a tune I have great affection for as I think my father would have been proud that I had made a tune specially for him. When I composed it I could imagine him playing his accordion and it feels like a tune I have known all my life. I sent Alwyn Tait a copy of 'Da New Ferries' when I first composed it and his comment was that it sounded a bit like the Ian Burns style. I took that as a great compliment as having had a few sessions with Ian, I became a great admirer of his compositions. Ian was a man who could play a multitude of instruments including the bagpipes.

I mentioned my father – known everywhere as Dollar, proper name Alexander – he was my first real teacher although my lessons were somewhat sporadic and unorthodox. He most likely gave me lessons to begin with because my mother kept nagging him. I suppose like most young boys I wouldn't do scales, wouldn't learn to read music and was generally a law unto myself, thinking that if my father could play music there couldn't really be much to it. Although he did teach me to read music I found I could play from records and, having a good memory, just played what I heard. This made him angry and not being noted for his patience he would rant and rave about how I was ruining my ear and wasting money on records when I could buy hundreds of tunes in manuscript form. I suppose we had a normal father son relationship.

My uncle Harold, a very patient man when it came to music, taught me a lot about technique for which I am grateful today, but he only really came into the picture a bit later. He was a great lover of classical music and although he could play anything, classical music was his love. It was a rare treat when Harold and Dollar got together on accordion and fiddle as they could play in harmony. This made a good combination especially if a guitar was included. In his younger days Harold had a palm court orchestra and played at various venues around Lerwick. He also played in his father Gideon's family dance band with my father, Mrs Mustard and Magnus, was in the Lerwick Orchestra and worked full time. I suppose it's no wonder he never found time to get married.

Magnus James, or Jim to the family, was always in Yell when we were young as he was headmaster at Mid Yell school. Being the oldest of the three he got to go to university and become a teacher, so I only got to know him properly when he retired to Lerwick. When I moved to Peterhead I discovered he had started his teaching career at Peterhead Academy during the war and had been there when it was bombed by the Germans. It was there he met his wife Baba. Jim was a great piano player as well as a violin player. He also played organ in three Lerwick churches up until he was 90. Sadly he died in 2004 at the age of 93.

There are many more musicians who have had an influence on me and my music over the years, too many to mention without this turning into an autobiography. It should be remembered that most of the Shetland musicians I have mentioned here were busy holding down jobs in the community and their music making was something they did for the sheer love of it. This is how most of Scotland's best music came into being – ordinary people throughout the centuries composing, playing and arranging a variety of traditional sounds. The various instruments involved in this process have undoubtedly contributed greatly to the rich tapestry of styles and regional variations, leaving us with the rich legacy of priceless gems we have today. I personally feel these should be passed on for future generations to play and enjoy.

Thomas Gideon Stove

Elizabeth Slaven.

Jig

Alex o' Scarpness

Composed for Alexander John Stove

Alex is my oldest brother, Scarpness is the name of the croft in Sandwick where he and his wife Vivienne live. This tune has a bit of an Irish lilt to it because Alex is a great fan of the legendary Sean Maquire.

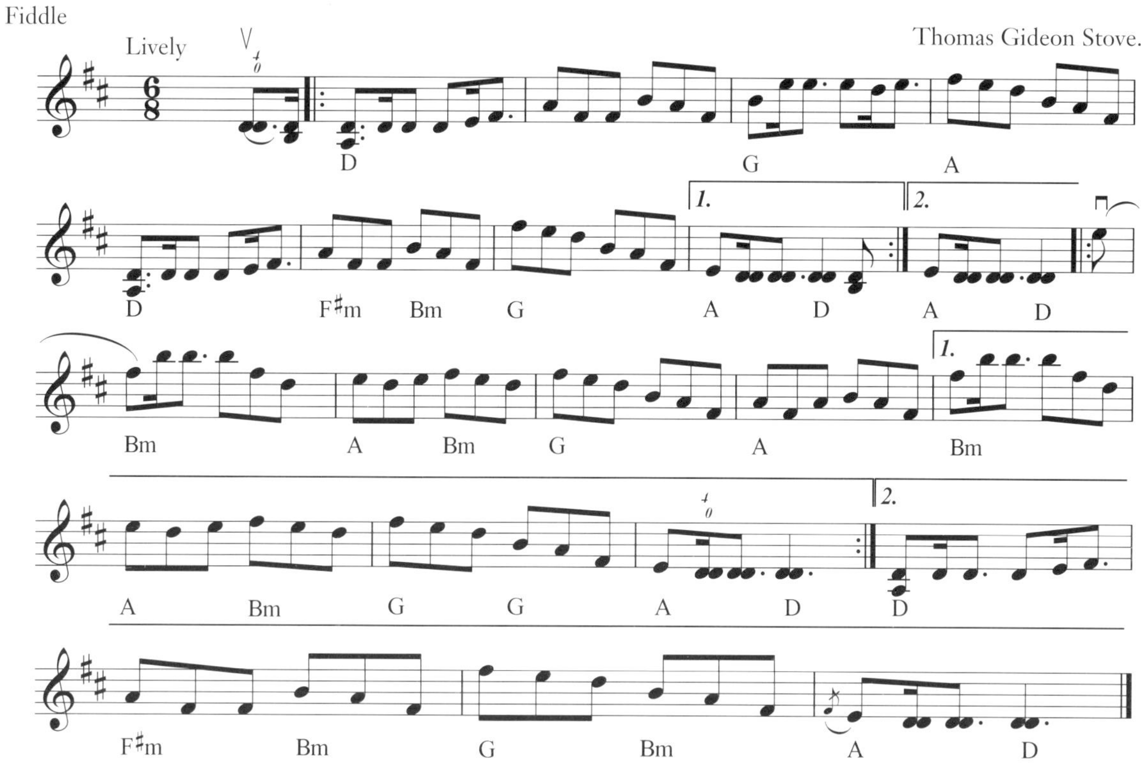

Alex Stove leads the band at Scarpness, Sandwick.

Coronation Hornpipe

This is a tune which came from a bundle of music manuscripts which belonged to my father and was among my books for years, he had either written it himself or had copied it. I would like to believe it was one of my grandfather Gideon Stove's tunes but it could just as easily be by uncle Harold or Magnus.

Unknown.

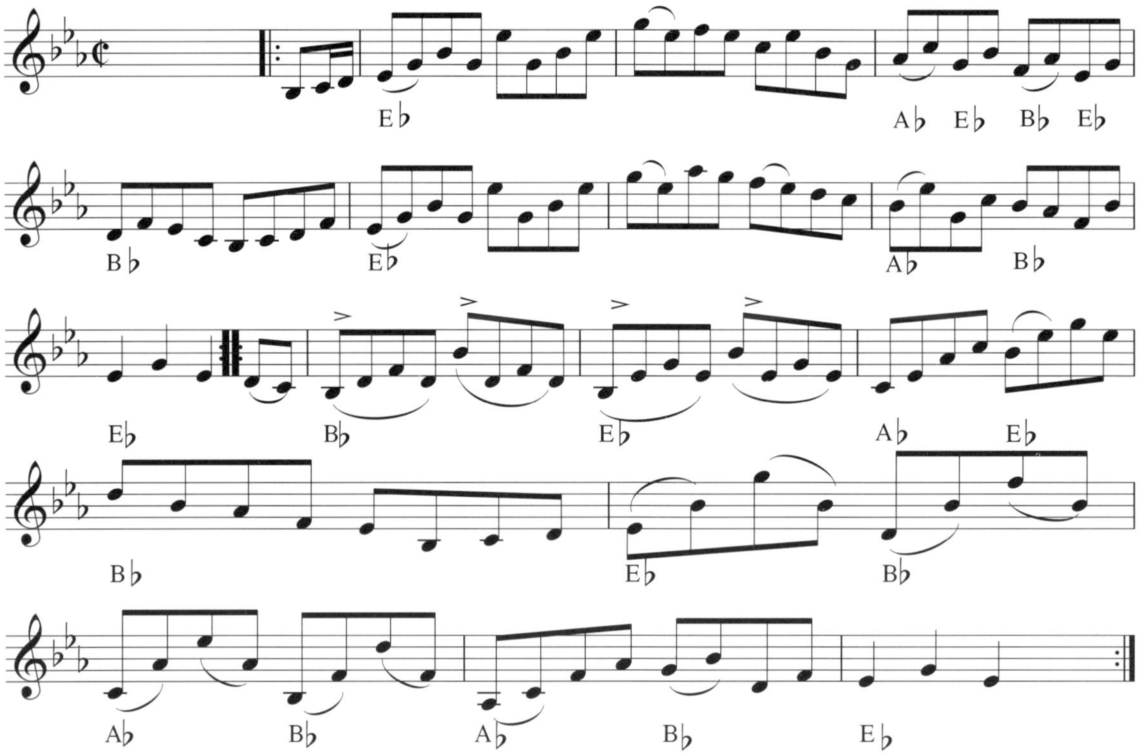

Shetland Reel

Da New Ferries

This is a tune I composed in celebration of the new north boats entering service on the Aberdeen to Shetland run. I can still recall my first ever trip on the *St Sunniva* to an army cadet camp in Orkney. We were certainly a sorry bunch of soldiers when we walked up Kirkwall pier in the morning.

Fiddle

Thomas Gideon Stove.

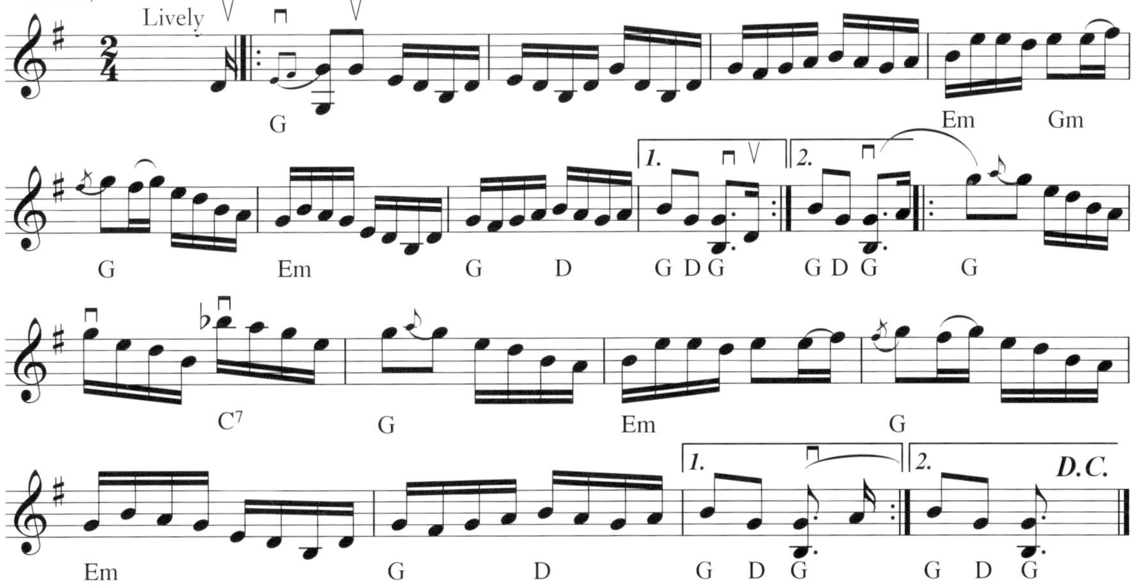

Jig

Da Peerie Green Man

This tune was just a bit of fun which reminded me of a Shetland poem I once made up while at Bells Brae primary school, much to the amusement of my then primary teacher Miss Pearson.

Thomas Gideon Stove.

Shetland Prose

Da Peerie Green Man

Ae' night as I was sittin ida peat fire glow
Wi da eerie shadow flittin roond aboot,
I heard dis peerie scruffle ben da hoose
laike a moose!
an hit wis comin fae da peat nuike.
I lookit ta see whit it coulda been
an ta my surprise I couldna believe me een,
a peerie man wis standin dairr
and wid you believe he wis green!
He said ta me he wid laik a grain a mait ta eat.
I said ta him, come "trow" ta me
an al gie dee gruel, wi an oat meal brunie,
an a cup o tae for bye.

I wrote this with my mother's help while at primary school.

Reel

Da Soond Sailor

This tune was specially composed for David Strachan, seaman, author and musician, Sound, Lerwick. Davie wrote a book recently which I read and enjoyed so much I thought I would pay him this compliment.

Lively

Thomas Gideon Stove.

Davy Strachan,
'Da Soond Sailor'
onboard S.S. Middlesex,
Sydney, Australia, 1959.

Two-step

Dollar's Box

Fiddle

Lively

Thomas Gideon Stove.

Dollar's Box

2

© Thomas G. Stove, 2003.

'Dollar's Box' is a tune dedicated to my late father, proper name Alexander Gideon Stove. Dollar played the 'box' as he called it – piano accordion to give it its Sunday name – from long before I was born.

It was only when I started to play fiddle that I realised how good a fiddle player and all round musician he was. He was a great lover of military two steps and big band music and played everything from jazz to Johann Strauss, classical music and Scottish dance music, you name it he would play it.

He began work in Lerwick Post office aged fourteen as a telegram boy and was there until he retired, only taking time out to serve in the RAF during the war. He reckoned he knew everybody in Shetland through his postal work, if not I am sure there were few in Shetland who didn't know him.

A. G. Stove and accordion. T. Stove in foreground c.1963 Up-Helly-A' squad 'Going Going Gone'.

Shetland Reel

Fiddler Up Da Rodd

Composed with Aly Bain in mind

Whenever I mention to people that I come from Lerwick they always say you must know Aly Bain. Aly lived just up the road from me, his father used to ask me to sing when we went guizing at Christmas.

Lively

Thomas Gideon Stove.

Reel

Frasers Granite

This tune I composed in honour of a stone mason I worked with in Aberdeen for a while, called Allan Fraser. He was a great fellow for making jokes and bringing the pompous down to earth with a bump. He had a distinctive laugh which was easily recognisable, I have tried to imitate it in the second section.

Thomas Gideon Stove.

Building granite at our garden.

Shetland Reel

I'll See the Isles in the Morning

I don't know what I was thinking when I composed this. It was just a bit of fun which I tried out with one of my pupils who is a fairly good musician. He liked it and wanted a copy so I made a variation for it.

Lively

Thomas Gideon Stove.

2

Thomas in Stromness.

Reel

Jacqui's Birnie Beau

Jacqui is my brother Billy's daughter who married a fellow called Duncan Grant from Birnie near Elgin. They now live in Aberdeenshire designing and making jewellery.

Thomas Gideon Stove.

© Thomas G. Stove, 2004.

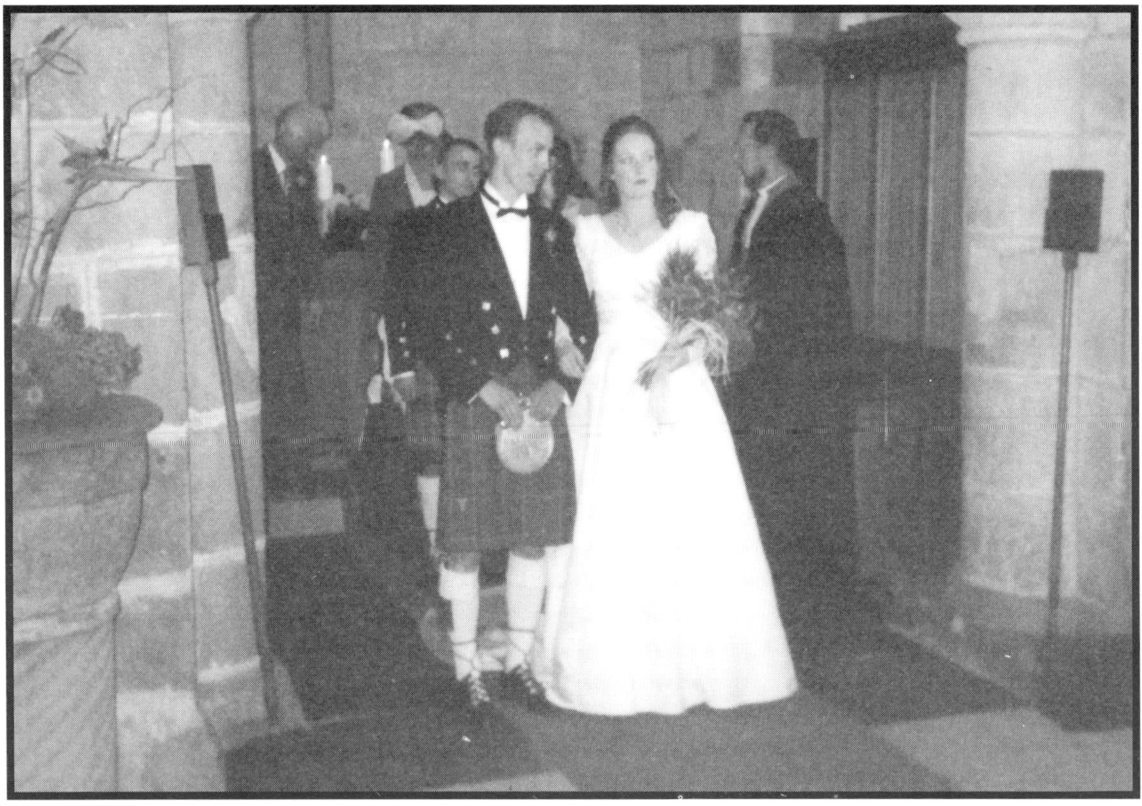

Jacqui's wedding, Elgin.

Shetland Reel

Larry Doon da Rope Locker

This is a tune I composed for an old school pal Larry Manson, who used to keep us all amused with his fishing tales. Larry spent his summer holidays from school working on a Whalsay herring drifter. When he left school Larry went straight to the fishing, married a Whalsay lass and settled in Whalsay. The rope locker was Larry's work place aboard, him being the youngest and smallest.

Thomas Gideon Stove.

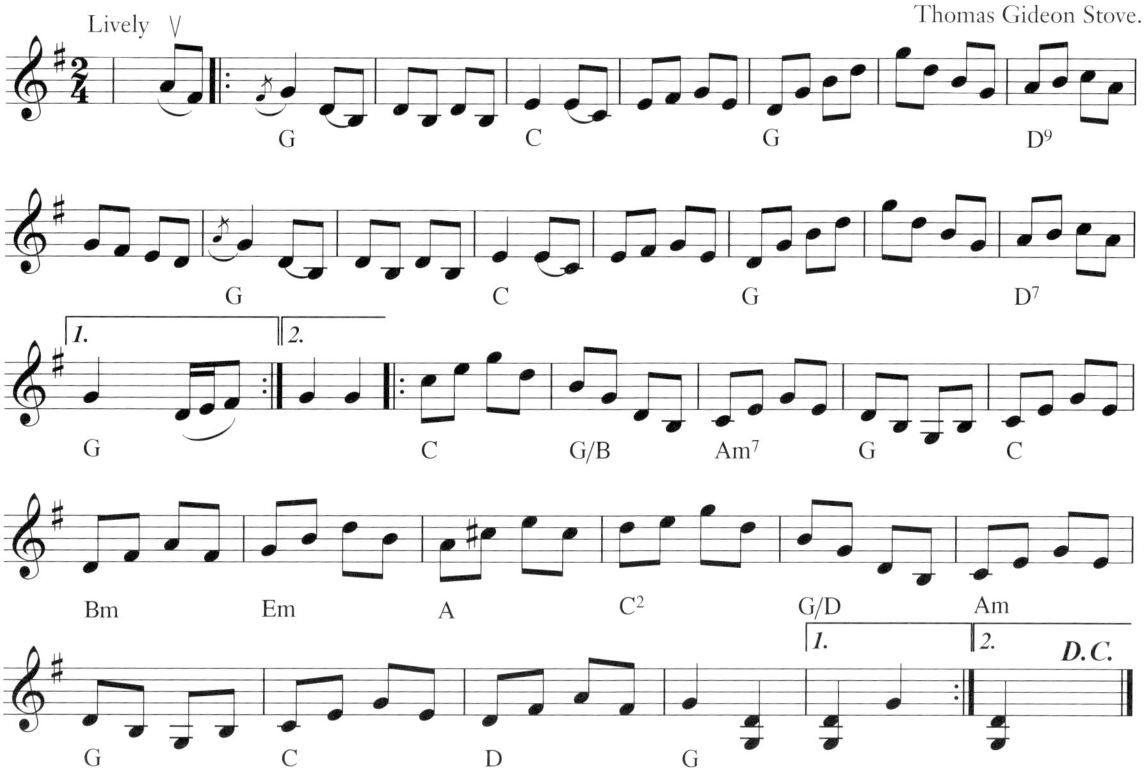

Larry's first boat, Brighter Morn.

Jig

Mattie's Dancing Pumps

Mattie, proper name Mathew Mckelvie, a college friend who plays fiddle, bagpipes and numourous other wind instruments, decided he would get his presentation across better to the class if he could show us the dance steps. A good job he did too, dressed in his kilt and of course a set of dancing pumps.

Lively

Thomas Gideon Stove.

Strathspey

Mrs Patricia Elaine Stove

Thomas Gideon Stove.

Mrs Patricia Elaine Stove.

Jig

Patty on the Rampage

This is one for my long suffering wife Pat, who came home while I was composing this and gave me a row for letting the fire go out – again!

Rhuaridh's Hornpipe

Composed for a neighbour's grandson who was only three years old at the time.

Lively

Thomas Gideon Stove.

Slow Air

Running for a Fry

I would forgive you if you thought 'Running for a Fry' should be a reel or a jig, but this tune came to me when I saw an old fishing boat stripped and beached on Bressay. It seemed so sad and alone. Then my mind started going back to childhood days when the herring drifters landed in Lerwick harbour, and how as boys in short breeks we used to run to the pier for a fry of herring, from a Burra or Whalsay boat.

A. Minor

Thomas Gideon Stove.

Karen's wedding.

Scottish Jig

Snowy Wedding

This is a tune written for my stepdaughter Karen's wedding. She married Mike and I gave her away. The wedding was in Cruden Bay and despite the horizontal snow a great night was had by all.

Tall ships, Lerwick.

A chat with Peerie Willie Johnson on the street.

Tall Ships Waltz

Composed by Alwyn Tait. Lerwick
Arrangement Thomas Gideon Stove.

Jig

Turfer's Skye Caravan

Tammy Irvine, my old pal and fellow fiddler, somehow picked up the title of Da Turfer. He hired a caravanette and did a tour of Scotland, including the isle of Skye. Tammy and his wife Margaret decided to pay us a visit and as they left this little tune came to me.

Trying out Tom's hardanga fiddle, Cunningsburgh.

The Michael Moar Jig

This is a jig I composed for an Aberdeen friend of mine who had a fiftieth birthday party not long ago. We had a nice musical evening and I wrote this for him when we got home. Michael is a great guitar and mandolin player.

Thomas Gideon Stove.

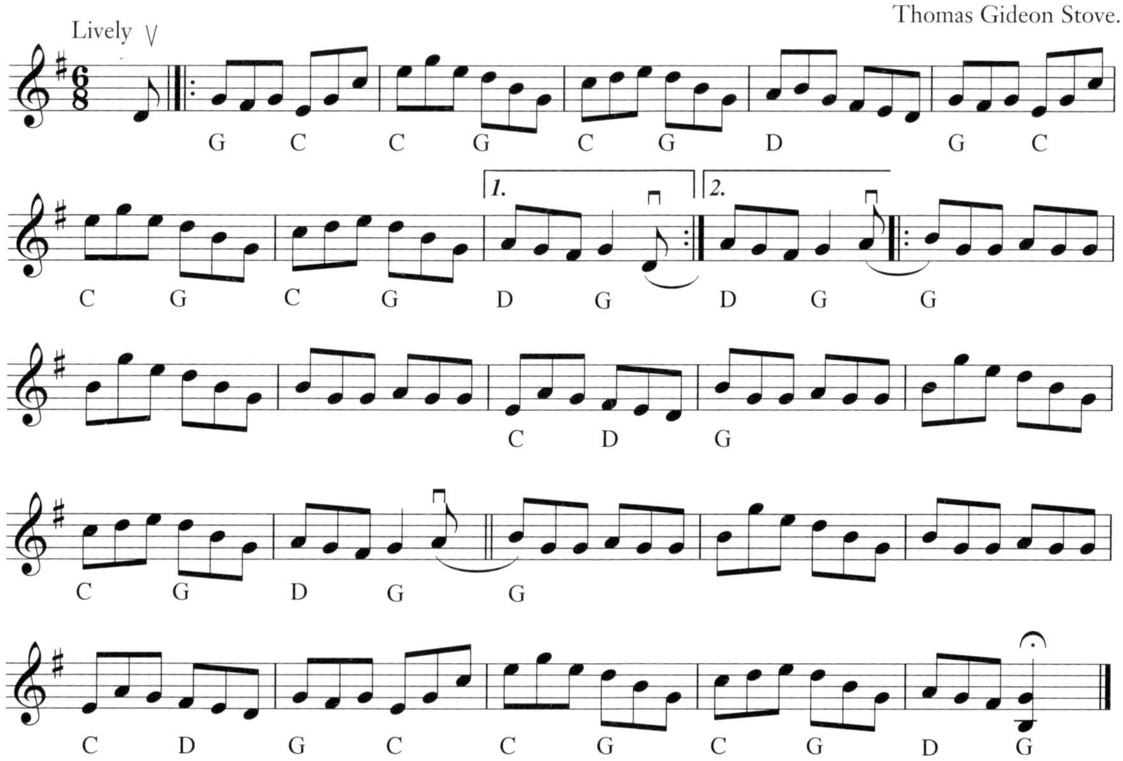

The Ramblers' Waltz

This tune was composed for my wife's sister Adeline and her husband John Cruickshank, both enthusiastic members of the Peterhead Ramblers Club.

Thomas Gideon Stove.

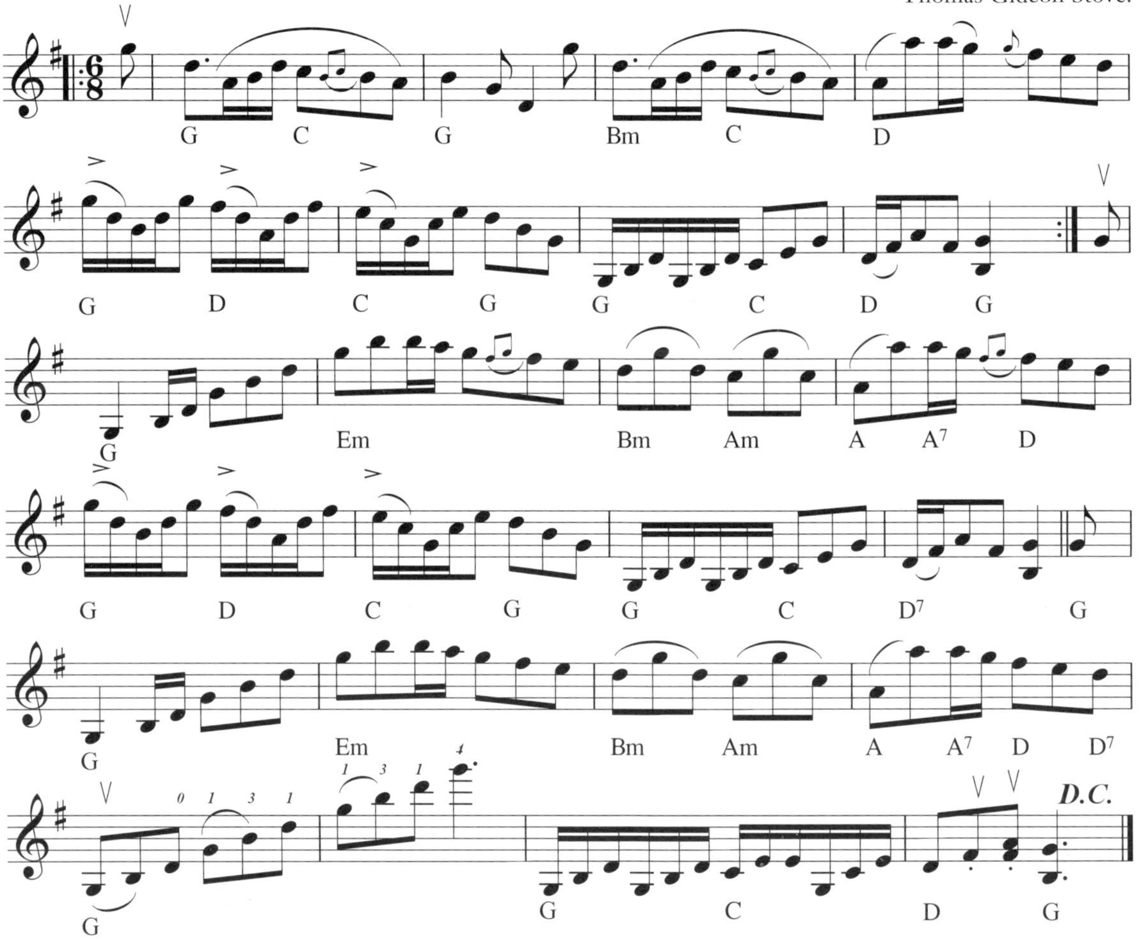

© Thomas G. Stove, 2003.

Some Peterhead ramblers.

Modern Scottish Reel

Tricker's Conundrum

Tim Tricker was a tutor at college with whom I got on very well. I asked him one day to give me some help writing this tune down on paper and he said "that's a bit of a conundrum", hence the title.

Thomas Gideon Stove.

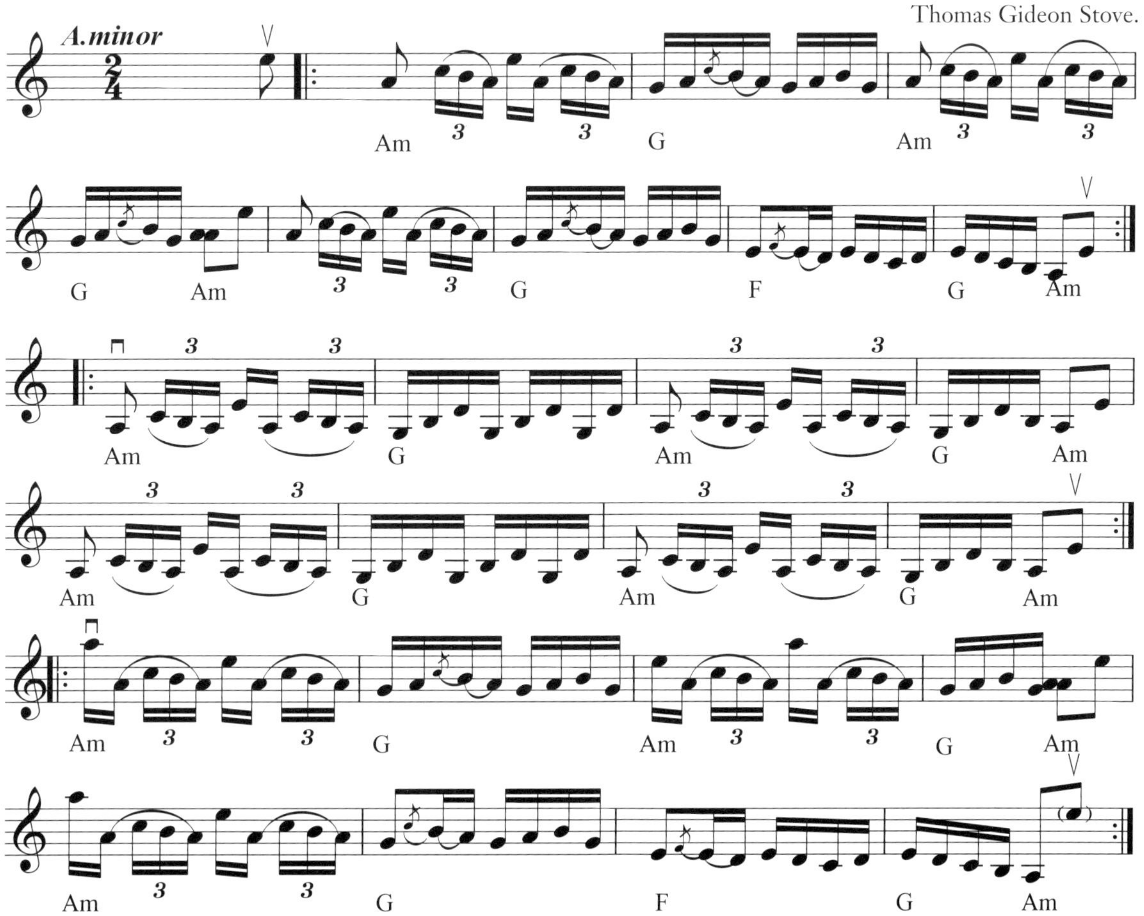

March

Tune for Alwyn

This tune was composed for Alwyn Tait of Lerwick, musician, composer and friend. Alwyn lived next door to my uncle Magnus James and was very helpful to him in his latter years.

Briskly Thomas Gideon Stove.

Alwyn Tait, 1946.

Shetland Reel

Twa Lumms Fliting

The twa lumms in this tune are the ones on Peterhead power station which can be seen from our house. The big one can be seen from miles away. I wrote this tune when the second one was being built. Thankfully the second chimney did not end up as high as the first, but as it was built I could imagine them arguing and fliting with each other as to who was biggest and best.

Lively

Thomas Gideon Stove.

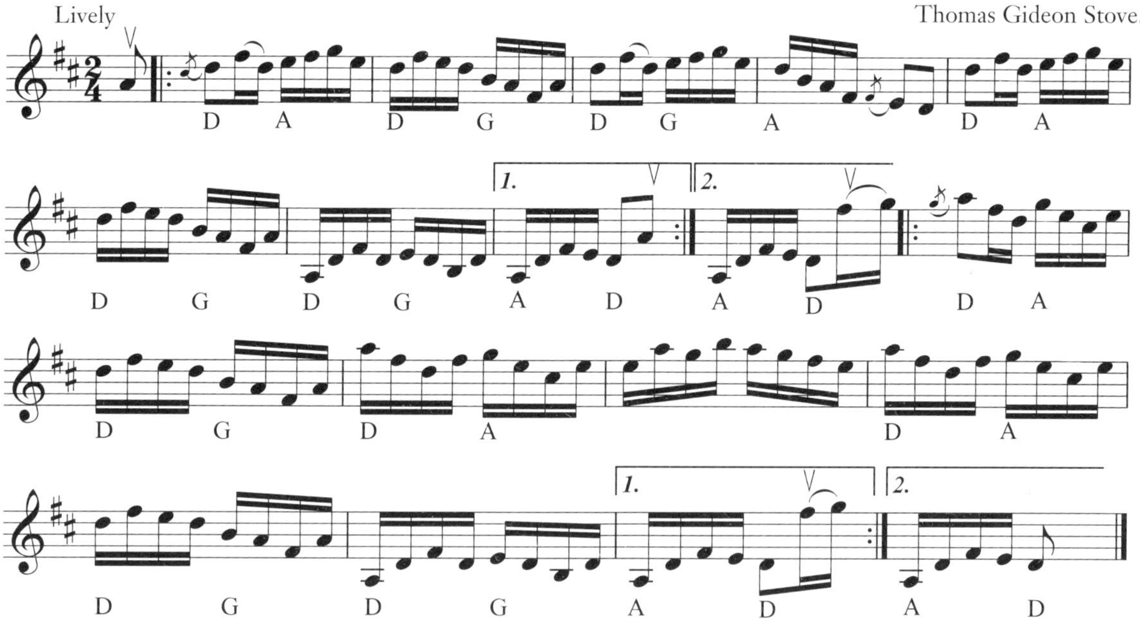

The power station as seen from our house.

Acknowledgements

To Mrs Elizabeth Slaven for her piano accompaniment on the CD and help sorting out the chords.

Mr John Slaven, Elizabeth's husband, for recording, producing and editing the CD and laying the original foundations for this project.

Mrs Vanda Mazzoleni, my college fiddle tutor, for her help with the chords, and all her kindness, patience and support over the years.

Mrs Charlotte Black of The Shetland Times, Lerwick for seeing this job through to the end.

Mr and Mrs John Cruckshank for the photo of Peterhead Ramblers.

Mr Alwyn Tait for permission to use his tune 'The Tall Ships' as an arrangement in my college course work and in this publication. For looking out the photo for 'Tune for Alwyn' and searching the Lerwick Museum for other photos.

Mr Larry Manson for finding me the photo of the *Brighter Morn.*

Mr Davy Strachan who gave the photograph for 'Da Soond Sailor'.

The Lerwick Museum for permission to use their photos.

The Peterhead Museum for permission to use the photo of the boy with the fry of herring.

Mr Paul Anderson – a sincere thanks for his kind foreword, it is much appreciated.

My wife Pat for her patience and understanding while I was doing all the composing, writing, research etc., and anyone else who I have inadvertently forgotten to mention.

Thank you one and all.

CD Listing

All the tunes on this CD are played individually for easy access in a learning situation.